READING
THE MAYA
GLYPHS

READING
THE MAYA
GLYPHS

MICHAEL D. COE · MARK VAN STONE

with glyph illustrations throughout

SECOND EDITION

The late Linda Schele was an inspiration to us both, and a calligraphic mentor to Mark. We therefore dedicate this volume to her memory.

Authors' note on the second edition

This revised edition incorporates the latest discoveries in hieroglyphic research, and incorporates new information and thinking on Classic Maya grammar and ancient spellings of Maya words. Where new readings of previously undeciphered glyphs have been verified (such as the true names for some rulers), they are included here.

Frontispiece: Lintel 8, Yaxchilan. See pages 92, 170–171.

All illustrations are by Mark Van Stone unless otherwise credited.

First published in the United States of America in 2001 by Thames & Hudson Inc., 500 Fifth Avenue, New York, New York 10110

thamesandhudsonusa.com

Second edition 2005
Reprinted 2015

Library of Congress Catalog Card Number 2004112870

ISBN 978-0-500-28553-4

Printed and bound in China by Hong Kong Graphics & Printing Ltd.

CONTENTS

PREFACE 7

1 THE CULTURAL BACKGROUND OF MAYA WRITING 11
1.1 Overview of a civilization 11
1.2 Scribes and artists 13
1.3 The language of the inscriptions 15

2 THE NATURE OF THE MAYA SCRIPT 17
2.1 Principles 17
2.2 Syllabograms 20
2.3 Morphosyllabic signs 22
2.4 Logograms with phonetic complements 24
2.5 Polyvalence 25
2.6 Conflation 26
2.7 Some grammar 26
2.7.1 *Nouns* 27
2.7.2 *Gender* 28
2.7.3 *Pronouns* 29
2.7.4 *Adjectives* 31
2.7.5 *Verbs* 32
2.8 Locative prepositions 35

3 TIME AND THE CALENDAR 37
3.1 General remarks 37
3.2 Maya numbers 38
3.3 The Calendar Round 40
3.3.1 *The 260-day Count* 41
3.3.2 *The Haab* 42
3.4 The Long Count and the Initial Series 45
3.4.1 *The Initial Series* 48
3.4.2 *The Supplementary Series* 49
3.5 Distance Numbers, Period Endings, and anniversaries 53

4 ROYAL LIVES AND ROYAL RITUALS 59
4.1 General remarks 59
4.2 Life-cycle events 59
4.2.1 *Birth* 59
4.2.2 *Accession* 61
4.2.3 *Death and burial* 62
4.3 Ritual activities 63
4.3.1 *Period Ending rites* 63
4.3.2 *Bloodletting* 64
4.3.3 *God impersonation* 65
4.3.4 *Royal dance* 65
4.3.5 *Ballplaying and ballcourts* 66
4.3.6 *Postscript* 67

5 PLACES AND POLITIES 68
5.1 Emblem Glyphs 68
5.2 Toponyms (place names) 71

6 DYNASTIC NAMES AND TITLES   74
    6.1   Titles   74
    6.2   Rulers   79

7 RELATIONSHIPS   86
    7.1   Parentage statements   86
    7.2   Spouse   87
    7.3   Siblings   88

8 WARFARE   89
    8.1   Glyphs for general war   89
    8.2   The taking of prisoners   90

9 SCRIBES AND ARTISTS   94
    9.1   Users of brush pens   94
    9.2   Carvers   95
    9.3   Other titles for artists and scribes   96

10 CERAMIC TEXTS   98
    10.1   General remarks   98
    10.2   The Primary Standard Sequence (PSS)   99

11 THE SUPERNATURAL WORLD   108
    11.1   General remarks   108
    11.2   Divinity and godhead   109
    11.3   The major gods   110
    11.4   Paired gods   118
    11.5   Triads   118
    11.6   The Death Gods   119
    11.7   The *way* spirit-companions   121

12 THE INANIMATE AND ANIMATE WORLDS   123
    12.1   The physical world   123
       12.1.1   *The directions*   123
       12.1.2   *The colors*   125
       12.1.3   *The sky and the earth*   126
    12.2   Humans   128
    12.3   Animals   129
    12.4   Buildings and structures   132
    12.5   Stone objects   133
    12.6   Pottery vessels   135
    12.7   Costume and personal adornment   135

Illustration Examples   137
Syllabary   155
A Maya Lexicon   161
Calendrical Formulae and Tables   167
Software Programs   168
Exercise Answers   169
Brief Bibliography   172
Acknowledgments   173
Index   174

PREFACE

Almost 160 years ago, the jungle-shrouded ruins of the ancient Maya civilization of Mexico and Central America were discovered by the American diplomat John Lloyd Stephens and his companion Frederick Catherwood, an English topographical artist. It was Stephens' hope that some Champollion would soon come along and decipher the strange hieroglyphs on the many carved monuments that they had encountered, but that was not to be. A century of intensive research on the glyphs resulted in the unraveling of the complex Maya calendar and astronomy, but *decipherment* – meaning the matching of signs to the language encoded in the script – was not to occur on any significant scale until the decade of the 1950s. Since then, there has been substantial progress, and it can now be said that we can actually read the majority of Maya texts, whether inscribed on stone or written in codices (books), in their original language.

That the Maya script is a somewhat difficult one, both in its underlying structure and in the way scribes rang variations on it, cannot be denied. Yet the subject matter of most public inscriptions, like those of ancient Egypt, is relatively restricted, and there is much repetition and redundancy. For the senior author, having visited the cities of the Nile armed with several "how to" pamphlets, and having derived much additional pleasure and understanding from being able to read royal names, dedications, and other matters important to the pharaohs, it struck him that a beginner's manual to the Maya glyphs could also be written. Our models here are Karl-Theodor Zauzich's excellent introduction to Egyptian writing, *Hieroglyphs without Mystery* (1992), and the more extensive (and intensive) *How to Read Egyptian Hieroglyphs* by Mark Collier and Bill Manley (1998). A brief pamphlet by the late Sir Eric Thompson, *Maya Hieroglyphs without Tears*, appeared in 1972, and while well illustrated, was hopelessly out of date even in the year of its publication.

As in Egypt, among the Maya there was a strong linkage between text and picture, one providing a commentary on the other, and the reader to whom this book is directed will be well rewarded when he or she discovers that relationship in a particular stela or tablet. The fact that a ruler or scribe who lived over a thousand years ago can speak to us across the gulf of time and space, and be understood, is a reward in itself.

We have presumed no previous knowledge of the Maya or their script. Our aim has been to take the reader step by step into decipherment, with examples taken from real texts. Our hope is that the amateur traveler visiting the Maya ruins, and perhaps even the beginning and intermediate student, will be able through this manual to read relatively simple texts, and to gain a deeper understanding of the remarkable civilization that produced them.

One of the problems in dealing with Maya writing is that of artistic license among the early scribes – in contrast to the situation with the Egyptian script, there can be no standardized font for the Maya glyphs since the scribes were free, within bounds, to use their imaginations on how they wrote particular glyphs, and were encouraged to do so by their royal patrons (*ill. 3:* see Illustration Examples pages 137–154). The junior author, Mark Van Stone, a trained calligrapher, has produced nearly all of the drawings in this book; for each and every glyph he has tried to find order in the variation, concentrating on the distinctive features which differentiate that sign from all others.

We would encourage the reader who would like to delve even deeper into the Classic and Post-Classic Maya to attend the Maya workshops, seminars, and weekend courses that are now given at several universities across the United States. The most venerable of these is the Maya Hieroglyphic Workshop at the University of Texas in Austin. Each of these sessions is open to registrants on any level of expertise, and attendees are furnished with Xeroxed handbooks that are themselves mines of information on both script and culture.

On page 168 we have included several programs and formulae for the calculation of Maya dates. Armed with these and with a hand calculator, the traveler to the land of the Maya ought to be able to handle most calendrical expressions; the stay-at-home student with a laptop or desk computer would be best served by any one of several excellent advanced programs which we have listed in the same appendix.

Pronunciation guide

The early Franciscan friars who came to the Maya realm with the Spanish conquistadores developed an orthography for writing the native languages – particularly Yukatek – alphabetically, and until recently this has remained in use among Maya scholars, with some slight modifications. However, during the 1980s a more modern orthography was promulgated by the Academy of Maya Languages in Guatemala, and this has become the standard for both linguists and epigraphers. It is the one that will be used here, with slight modification.

The vowels (*a, e, i. o, u*) are generally pronounced as they would be in Spanish. However, in most Mayan languages, including that of the Classic inscriptions, there is a distinction between long and short vowels; switching from one to the other can change the meaning of a word. Long vowels are marked by doubling, as in *baak*, "bone."

Another distinction made in Mayan is between non-glottalized and glottalized consonants. To pronounce the latter, the throat is constricted, with the result that such stops are accompanied by a very slight "explosion" of air. Glottalization is here indicated by an apostrophe ('). Examples of how meanings change with glottalization are:

chab, "earth, bee"	*ch'ab*, "create, to fast"
kan, "snake"	*k'an*, "yellow"

Incidentally, linguists tell us that all *b*s in the language are actually glottalized (i.e. *chab'*, rather than *chab*), but since that trait makes no change in the meaning of words with *b*, and in the interests of simplicity, it will not be recognized in this book. It is also true that whenever a vowel begins a Mayan word, this is preceded by a glottal stop, but this is also the case in English (such as before the *a* in *apple*), and we see no need to confuse the reader with further apostrophes – there are quite enough here already!

There are two voiceless aspirates in Classic Mayan (the language recorded in the Maya inscriptions). One is *h*, very similar to English *h*; the other is *j*, a guttural consonant like the *j* in Spanish *jarabe*, or the *ch* in German *Bach*. The *x* consonant is used to record a sound like English *sh*. The weak consonants *y* and *w* are sometimes used as glides from one vowel to another.

In the early stages of the decipherment, it was thought that the ancient Maya scribes could only approximate the sounds of their language in the script. We now realize that the Maya writing system was extremely advanced in how it recorded not only the phonetic distinctions described above, but also fine nuances of their complex grammar. In the hands of their specialists, it was a highly sophisticated and supple instrument to express whatever they wanted to say.

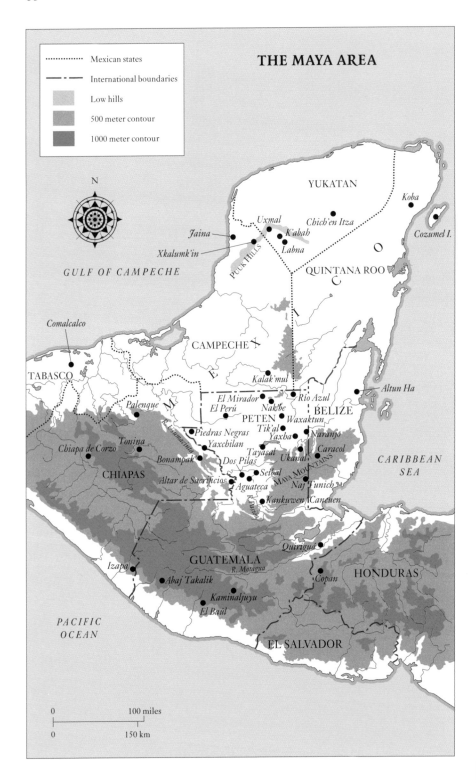

THE MAYA AREA

Mexican states

International boundaries

Low hills

500 meter contour

1000 meter contour

N

YUKATAN

Koba

Uxmal   Chich'en Itza

Jaina   K'abah   Cozumel I.

Xkalumk'in   Labna

GULF OF CAMPECHE   PUUK HILLS   QUINTANA ROO

Comalcalco

CAMPECHE

TABASCO   Kalak'mul

Altun Ha

El Mirador   Río Azul

Palenque   El Perú   Nak'be   BELIZE

PETEN   Waxaktun

Piedras Negras   Tik'al

Chiapa de Corzo   Tonina   Yaxchilan   Yaxha   Naranjo

Bonampak   Dos Pilas   Tayasal   Ukanal   Caracol   CARIBBEAN

CHIAPAS   Altar de Sacrificios   Seibal   MAYA MOUNTAINS   SEA

Aguateca   Naj Tunich

Kaukuwen   Cancuen

Quirigua

GUATEMALA

Izapa   R. Motagua

Abaj Takalik   Copan   HONDURAS

Kaminaljuyu

El Baúl

PACIFIC
OCEAN

EL SALVADOR

0 ——— 100 miles

0 ——— 150 km

1

THE CULTURAL BACKGROUND OF MAYA WRITING

1.1 Overview of a civilization

Maya civilization arose, flourished, and died in the tropical lowlands of south-eastern Mexico and neighboring Central America. While earlier writing systems are known outside the Maya area proper, the first fully fledged Maya inscriptions appeared before AD 250 in the Peten region of northern Guatemala, initiating the Classic period of Maya history. Between then and about AD 900, we have many hundreds of texts on stone monuments, dated in the Long Count system (to be described in **3.4**); but by the 9th century city after city ceased to put up such records as the southern Maya lowlands were progressively abandoned to the encroaching forest. This marks the great collapse, and the demise of Classic culture.

Nonetheless, in the northern Maya area (Yukatan), the 9th century saw a brief resurgence of complex civilization in what is known as the Terminal Classic, with the rapid rise to power of Chich'en Itza, one of the largest and most powerful cities of ancient Mesoamerica, with a large body of extremely important inscriptions. Whether Chich'en's hegemony over Yukatan, and perhaps beyond, lasted into the subsequent Post-Classic period (AD 900 until the Conquest) is still hotly debated, but what is not in doubt is the rarity or even non-existence of Post-Classic stone texts there and elsewhere in the lowlands. However, scribes surely continued to write on bark-paper books and on other perishable materials; in fact, it is from this period that all four of the extant Maya codices have survived.

Thanks to the modern decipherment, we now have a fairly accurate picture of Classic Maya society and politics. Although some of the largest cities, particularly Tik'al and Kalak'mul, at times achieved a degree of control over some of the others through a combination of military might and diplomacy, the Maya landscape was dotted with a number of usually-independent city-states, each with a capital city and rather fluid borders. At the head of each such city-state was a hereditary ruler or *k'uhul ajaw* ("holy king"), along with his wife or wives, family, and a large court. Beneath him were one or more individuals distinguished by the title *sajal*; these seem to have acted not only as military chiefs but as provincial governors. The king himself and his retinue, along with a vast number of servants, resided in a stone-built palace with many vaulted rooms. All sorts of rituals, ceremonial dances, and sacrifices were carried out in the confines of the palace and its courtyards, and in nearby ancestral temples raised on tall, stepped pyramids. In almost any city of sufficient size were one or more masonry ballcourts, in which a richly symbolic game was played with a rubber ball.

A great deal of tension existed between these rival states, and warfare eventually became endemic, especially in the 8th century AD; the primary goal of these conflicts seems to have been the taking of high-ranking captives for sacrifice, rather than territorial gain. Nonetheless, through force of arms, diplomatic visits, and royal marriages, two powerful rival kingdoms – Tik'al and Kalak'mul – managed to become "superpowers," with considerable military and political sway in the Late Classic southern Maya lowlands.

Within the royal family, the focus of attention was the king himself, his principal queen (*ix ajaw*), his heir apparent, and his ancestors. There is little doubt from the inscriptions and iconography that the royal line of some states was considered to be of divine origin, and sovereigns prefaced their personal names with the epithet of the Sun God. Maya kings were also identified with the Maize God, especially after death, and with this deity's offspring Hun Ajaw (Hunahpu, one of the Hero Twins in the post-Conquest *Popol Vuh*, the K'iche' sacred book). Allied with the royal family was a large, hereditary nobility, from whom the major administrative and military officers were probably drawn. The bulk of the population, however, was made up of farmers and artisans. At the very bottom were slaves, perhaps largely captives taken in war.

Classic Maya religion was thoroughly polytheistic, with a vast array of gods and spirits to be worshiped by all classes. Heading the pantheon was the aged Creator God Itsamnaaj, but equally important were Chaak, the bringer of rain and lightning, and K'awiil, the snake-footed patron of the royal house. Depictions on monuments often show the ruler brandishing a scepter in the shape of K'awiil. For some of those at the top of the social pyramid – royalty and probably the higher nobility – an individual was spiritually allied with a *way*, a goblin-like, chimaeric being that acted as a kind of spirit-companion or alter-ego for elite personages. Such creatures are frequently represented on elite polychrome and carved ceramics. In the centers of the great Maya cities, there were major calendrically-set ceremonies, such as those marking the anniversaries of royal accessions or the conclusion of major time periods like the 20-year katuns and 5-year tuns. The cult of the royal ancestors was powerful, and many of the grandest ceremonies were related to it. Particularly important in such rites was the putative (or real) founder of the dynasty. At Copan, this individual was a foreigner, perhaps from central Mexico, named Yax K'uk' Mo'; over his 5th-century tomb was erected a succession of temples dedicated to his memory, the last being so tall that it towered far above the rest of the buildings in the city's "acropolis."

1.2 Scribes and artists

To the pre-Conquest Maya, writing and painting were virtually identical, the single word *tz'ib* describing both actions. Nonetheless, the Maya did distinguish between the scribe (*aj tz'ib*) who used the brush pen and the scribe who carved or incised texts and scenes. From glyphic signatures appearing on monuments and on pictorial vases we know the names and titles of a fair number of Late Classic scribes, who appear to have occupied an exalted position in Maya society; some, at least, were actually members of the royal family. Within the palace, the highest scribal rank was apparently that of *aj k'uhuun*, "the keeper of the holy paper"; an individual with many responsibilities – these may have included those of royal librarian, historian, genealogist, tribute recorder, marriage arranger, master of ceremonies, and (with more certainty) astronomer and mathematician. On those scribes who had attained high reputation was bestowed the honorary title of *aj itz'aat*, with the meaning "wise one."

The scribes had their own gods, above all the twin Monkey-men known to us from a myth recorded in the *Popol Vuh;* these had been enemies of their half-brothers the Hero Twins, and in revenge were changed into monkeys through trickery. Among the other scribal deities was the quadripartite "Pawahtuun," an aged divinity who held up the earth and the heavens, and who presided over the end of the year.

While no Classic books have survived, depictions on pottery indicate that they were common in the period. Like the four extant Post-Classic manuscripts, these were screenfolds, written with quill and brush pens on bark paper coated with burnished white gesso, and are depicted with jaguar-skin covers, perhaps indicating that they were royal books. Basic to the production of texts on both books and monuments was the laying out of a network of red guidelines, within which the glyphs were to be painted or carved, made necessary by the tradition of reading these from left to right and top to bottom in exactly paired columns.

Maya writing appears on an impressive array of materials, and in many places: on carved stone stelae, door lintels, and panels, in carved architectural stuccos (*ill. 11*), within painted murals, and carved or incised on pottery vases and bowls (*ills. 14, 15*). Some of the most exquisite calligraphy has been found on carved jades, bones (*ill. 12*), and shells, extremely precious objects included as offerings in elite tombs and graves. Many texts must have been on wood, but apart from the famous carved lintels of Tik'al (*ill. 10*), few of these have survived the elements.

Throughout the Classic, and in the Post-Classic codices, pictures and texts were as closely linked as they were among the ancient Egyptians: the texts inform the pictures, and the pictures the texts, a circumstance which has often aided decipherment, and conversely, has led to the understanding of the otherwise mysterious actions and objects depicted by the artist.

How widespread was literacy among the ancient Maya? Although this question is very difficult to answer, it is usually assumed that this was confined to a very select few. However, one should keep in mind that in all known writing systems, especially those with a logophonetic basis (based on both meaning signs and sound signs, as is the case with Mayan, Egyptian, and Chinese), it is far easier to read such a script than to write it. In fact, most of the great Classic carved monuments were displayed in public places, and were obviously meant to be read by more than a narrow group of elite scribes and bureaucrats. And, finally, as the success of various Maya workshops held in recent years in several American cities has proved, a rough-and-ready reading knowledge of the script may be gained by relative neophytes within the space of a single week! Of course, all of this is helped by the fact that Classic monumental texts are fairly limited in subject matter, and that they are accompanied by pictures that help out in their interpretation.

Long ceramic texts are an entirely different matter, and give hints of the subtlety and complexity of what may have once been contained in the now-disappeared Maya books of the Classic period. We now recognize that some of these texts actually record real speech – first-person statements, and dialogues between two personages. But they are definitely *not* for beginners!

1.3 The language of the inscriptions

For almost a century it was assumed by scholars that ancient Maya texts, both in the codices and in the inscriptions, were written in Yukatek Maya, the dominant tongue of the northern Yukatan Peninsula. This assumption was placed in doubt by the late Sir Eric Thompson, who in 1950 suggested, on the basis of the Colonial-period distribution of languages belonging to the Mayan family, that the scribes of the southern lowlands wrote in some form of Ch'olan (although he continued to believe that the codices were in Yukatek). Languages belonging to the western branch of Ch'olan include Ch'ol proper, still spoken in the vicinity of Palenque, Chiapas – this tongue, or an ancestral form of it, has been favored by several specialists as the language of the inscriptions.

More recently, the tide has turned in favor of some form of *Eastern* Ch'olan, with one extinct member, Ch'olti', and one surviving one, Ch'orti', still spoken by thousands of villagers in a region lying astride the Guatemala-Honduras border (significantly, not far from the Classic city of Copan). An important paper by the linguist John Robertson and the epigraphers Stephen Houston and David Stuart has proved that the hieroglyphic language was indeed an earlier form of Ch'olti' and Ch'orti' that will be here called "Classic Mayan." For over a thousand years this was the preferred literary language of the Maya scribes, even in the Post-Classic of the northern lowlands, for it had taken on the same degree of prestige that Middle Egyptian had in Late Dynastic Egypt, or Sumerian in Mesopotamia, or Latin in Medieval Europe, or Sanskrit in India, or Literary Chinese in China. Like these, while it may have begun as a vernacular, eventually Classic Mayan had evolved into a language that was mainly for reading and writing, rather than for everyday speech.

All of the 31 extant members of the Mayan language family, along with Classic Mayan, are grammatically very different from the languages (all belonging to the Indo-European family) that we either know as native speakers, or from having studied them in school. For one thing, there is no gender at all, for instance no such words or parts of words as "he" as opposed to "she," or "his" vs. "hers" or "its." Furthermore, Mayan languages make important distinctions which European ones hardly recognize, such as between pronouns associated with **intransitives** (verbs that have a subject but do not take an object) and those with **transitives** (verbs that have both a subject *and* an object); in fact, there are two entirely separate sets of pronouns, one to go with the former, and the other with the latter. Even further, the pronoun system for the subject of transitive verbs is essentially the same as that for possessives – linguists call this **ergativity,** and that for the subject of intransitive verbs is identical to that for the object of transitive ones. As the linguist James Fox has noted, it is as if one were to say in English "*my* father" (possessive) and "*my* shot the turkey" (transitive subject), but "*his* struck *me*" (transitive object) and "*me* slept" (intransitive subject).

In addition, to the time element of speech (what we would call **tense,** that is, past, present, and future), the Mayan languages add **aspect;** this consists of prefixes to action verbs that indicate whether the action is 1) completed, 2) not yet completed or still going on, and 3) something that will happen in the future. As if to add to the unfamiliarity of Mayan grammar, there is also present in Ch'olan and Yukatekan a special class of intransitive verbs and suffixes known as **positionals**, which express the physical environment or position of the actor or acted upon – such as sitting, standing, being face up or face down, etc. We shall come across these in the inscriptions.

The Mayan languages, like many others in the New World, are **polysynthetic**: a word will consist of a root stem, often of the CVC (consonant-vowel-consonant) sort, preceded and/or followed by various grammatical affixes, and will sometimes express what among English-speakers would be a complete sentence. Regarding syntax structure, the usual word order of transitive sentences with verbs and nouns varies among the different members of the family, but in Classic Mayan, as we shall see, it is verb-object-subject (VOS to linguists).

Daunting though all this sounds, the would-be neophyte decipherer should take heart from the fact that only a relatively small part of this complex grammar appears in the hieroglyphic texts, due to the restricted and somewhat stilted nature of the Classic inscriptions on stone. If we had in hand some or all of the thousands of books that must have been written during the Classic period, we would have an entirely different story!

2

THE NATURE OF THE MAYA SCRIPT

2.1 Principles

Maya texts, even those in the codices (books), are usually laid out within an imaginary right-angled grid like a chessboard. The resulting glyph blocks were generally written, and are to be read by us, from left to right and top to bottom, in paired columns. Thus if we designate the columns by the letters A, B, C, D, etc., and the horizontal rows as 1, 2, 3, 4, etc., the reading order would be A1, B1, A2, B2, A3. Once the bottommost glyph in column B is reached, the reader moves up to C1 and D1, and so forth. To be sure, there are exceptions to this rule, such as the single glyph columns and L-shaped or completely horizontal glyph rows that often appear on pottery, for example. A few very rare monumental and ceramic texts are to be read from right to left, or even in circular fashion, as on some stone altars. But we stress that the basic order is left to right, and top to bottom.

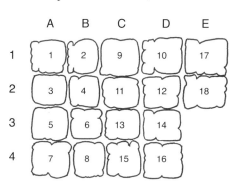

Probably because of the nature of the grid, individual glyphs are somewhat square, with rounded corners – an early French scholar called them "pebble-shaped." Some of these are relatively simple, consisting of a single sign, but most are compound, containing more than one significant element. The largest of the elements within the compound is called the **main sign**, while the smaller ones attached to it are termed **affixes**, but there is no uniform, truly functional difference between the two as far as the reading is concerned. There is, however, a general **reading order** for the signs in compound glyphs; this more-or-less follows the left-to-right, top-to-bottom rule, as in the following:

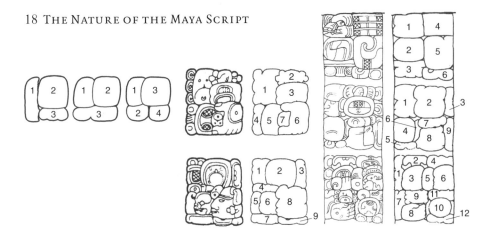

Nonetheless, this rule was often violated by the ancient scribes, for reasons that might be aesthetic, but which might also be imposed by cultural values (for example, placing the affixes which together read *ajaw*, "king," ▨▨ at the top rather than the bottom of a glyph compound ▨▨ ; in the same way Egyptian scribes positioned gods' names at the beginning of inscriptions, rather than where they "should" be). Everything that we know about the Classic scribes makes it clear that they were given a very wide latitude to play around with the script, as long as they conformed closely to the phonetics, grammar, and syntax of the underlying language.

Maya writing has both a semantic dimension and a phonetic one: some signs indicate meaning alone, while others express particular sounds in the language being recorded. In this it is similar to other ancient scripts, such as Egyptian, Chinese, and the cuneiform system of Mesopotamia. We call the "meaning" signs **logograms**; these stand for whole words or word-stems. For a list of the most common logograms in use among the Classic Maya, see pages 161–166. The phonetic signs are **syllabograms**, representing syllables (combinations of consonants and vowels), as well as the "pure vowels" (*a, e, i, o, u*) unaccompanied by any consonant. Maya writing is thus **logosyllabic**. It is no accident that there is no known script in the world, ancient or modern, which entirely consists of logograms – there would simply be far too many discrete signs for anyone to memorize, and too much ambiguity inherent to such a system.

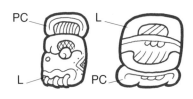

Accordingly, the scribes of these early civilizations attached signs known as **phonetic complements** (PC) to logograms (L) to help in their reading. Maya syllabograms were used in just such a way, as we shall see.

Yet, in the Maya system, any word that could be spelled with a logogram alone, or by a logogram with one or more phonetic complements, could and often *was* written purely syllabically (we shall examine the rules for this in **2.2**). So why didn't they give up the clumsy logograms, and write everything phonetically with syllabograms? The probably answer is that the Maya elite, including the scribes, put a high value on signs which not only had deep cultural meanings, but which could be relatively difficult to write (at least for neophytes).

SOME CONVENTIONS FOR TRANSCRIBING MAYA GLYPHS

A **transcription** is a more-or-less accurate record in Roman letters of the values of individual signs in a Maya glyph or text, each sound being separated from its neighbors by hyphens. Transcriptions will always be in boldface type, with **LOGOGRAMS** in upper case, and **syllabograms** in lower case. Parentheses around a vowel means that it is not pronounced. Here is an example:

po-p(o)-TUUN-n(i)

A **transliteration**, always in *italics*, represents actual Maya language (Classic Mayan) recorded in the glyphic original and/or its transcription. Example:

po-p(o)-TUUN-n(i) *pop tuun*

A **translation**, always in quotes and regular type, is the English-language version of a Classic Mayan transcription. An example of all three together:

po-p(o)-TUUN-n(i) *pop tuun* "stone mat"

Altogether, the Maya script contains approximately 800 signs or glyphs, among which only about 400 to 500 were in common use among the scribes (by contrast, there are over 12,000 signs or "characters" in Chinese, and a literate person knows at least 5,000 of these). Within the complete Maya signary, the majority of glyphs are logograms, many of which will be fully deciphered only when syllabic substitutions are identified.

2.2 Syllabograms

In the 16th century, the first bishop of Yukatan, Diego de Landa, described the Maya writing system in his *Relación de las Cosas de Yucatán* ("Account of the Affairs of Yukatan"). According to him, the natives wrote by means of what he claimed was an "alphabet," and he presented 29 such signs, with their supposed Spanish letter equivalents. After almost a century of fruitless attempts to decipher the Maya script by means of this "alphabet," a great breakthrough was reached in 1952 when the Russian scholar Yuri V. Knorosov recognized that what Landa had given was really a list of syllabograms. In his article, Knorosov laid out some of the rules by which the ancient Maya wrote with these syllabic signs. By now the known body of such signs has grown to include more than 150. Some of these are just variations on a theme, while many are **allograms** (alternate spellings) for one and the same sound syllable. The **syllabic grid** or **syllabary** can be found on pages 155–160; it is arranged so that the consonants are in a horizontal line at the top, and the vowels in a vertical column at the left. Although some of the possible positions (boxes) are now blank, future research may well fill these. The reader will be referring to this syllabary throughout this book, and we recommend that a Xerox copy be made and kept at hand.

The first and basic rule established by Knorosov is that to express a root of the consonant-vowel-consonant (CVC) sort – the commonest word type in the ancient language – the Maya scribe wrote it with two syllabograms, each standing for a consonant followed by a vowel (CV), with the sound of the second vowel suppressed. Knorosov's second rule is that of **synharmony**: the vowel of the second syllabogram usually should match the vowel of the first.

ku-ch(u) *kuch* "burden"

tzu-l(u), *tzul* "dog"

1 jo-ch'(o),
2 jo-ch'a *joch'* "drill"

 pi-tz(i) *pitz* "play ball"

Likewise, as we shall see, there should be a match between the vowel of a phonetic complement in final position and that of the logogram to which it is affixed. However, the rule of synharmony is far from ironclad. Actually, the final, silent vowel is **disharmonic** as often as it is synharmonic; this disharmony indicates that the vowel of the preceding syllable is **complex**, for instance long rather than short; since many Mayan dictionaries, especially the colonial ones, do not make note of vowel length, this nicety of scribal practice has only been detected in recent years. Disharmony also takes place when the root vowel takes an aspirate *h*, or even a glottal stop.

 ba-k(i) *baak* "prisoner"   tu-p(a) *tuup* "earspool"

 mu-t(i) *muut*, "bird, omen"

 a-k(u) *ahk* "turtle"   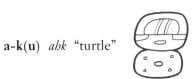 HAAB-b(i) *haab* "year"

A rare but significant feature of syllabic spelling is that two dots may be placed next to a syllabogram to indicate that it is to be repeated, thereby saving space. The best-known example of this is in some occurrences of the glyph for cacao or chocolate:

 ka-ka-w(a) *kakaw* "cacao," "chocolate"

EXERCISE 1

Using the syllabic grid (pages 155–160), transcribe the following (make sure you put parentheses around the silent final vowel):

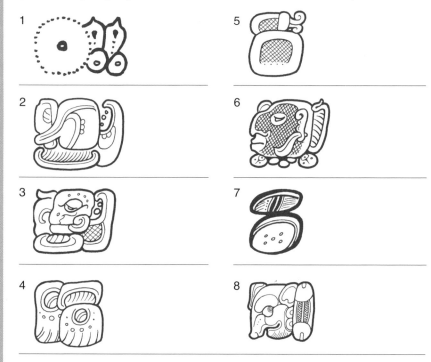

Answers on page 169

2.3 Morphosyllabic signs

Houston, Stuart, and Robertson have recently recognized a class of signs that bridge the categories of syllabogram and logogram. Here these will be called "morphosyllabic signs" (the more correct term "morphosyllabograms" sounds too unwieldy!).

- These are always word-final (i.e. suffixes).
- They always express meaning, particularly inflection; in a sense they are logographic and thus are written in uppercase bold letters.
- They "flip" the sound of a particular syllabic sign from the usual CV order to VC – that is, one is the mirror image of the other (e.g. **li** to **-IL**).
- They suspend the rule of disharmony – that is, the vowel of the preceding syllable may not necessarily be long even when it is not echoed by the vowel of the morphosyllabic sign that follows it.

Glyph	Reading	Origin	Usual function
	-AJ	ja	Suffix for passive verbs, present tense
	-AL	la	Adjectival suffix
	-AW	wa	Turns transitive verbs into intransitives; suffix for transitive verbs with Set A pronouns (see **2.7.3** below)
	-EY	ye	Early Classic version of **-iiy** (past tense) suffix
	-IB	bi	Instrumental suffix
	-IJ	ji	Root intransitive (present tense) suffix
	-IL	li	Abstractive suffix; ending for possessed objects
	-IS	si	Nominalizer

The various applications of these will be explained in the section on grammar (**2.7**). For the moment, let's look at **-IB**, a morphosyllabic sign with several functions. When attached to a verbal root, it acts as an instrumental suffix, allowing that event to take place, as in:

CHUM-m(u)-IB *chumib* "sit" + suffix = "place for sitting"

A far more common morphosyllabic sign is **-IL**. This can express an abstractive suffix that transforms a specific noun into its abstract form (somewhat similar to the suffixes *-ness* or *-ship* in English), for example:

ti-sa-ja-l(a)-IL *ti sajalil* "in the subordinate lordship"

Here the noun *sajal* is a term for a subordinate lord or governor. -IL also appears at the end of expressions indicating possessed objects: when objects are possessed, they take both a Set A pronoun (see **2.7.3**), that is **ni**, **a[w]**, **u**, or **ka**, and the suffix -IL.

 u-K'UH-IL *u-k'uhil* "it is his god"

It might be thought from the above that morphosyllabic signs are derived from syllabograms, but Houston feels that the opposite might be the case, since they appear so early in the history of the Maya script, when syllabic signs are barely to be discerned. We should also say here that there is still controversy among epigraphers about the nature of these signs, a testimony to the "fine-tuning" that the study of Maya writing is now undergoing at the hands of scholars.

2.4 Logograms with phonetic complements

To aid in their reading, logograms are usually accompanied by one or more syllabograms; as a rule, these latter are added as affixes to the main sign. The syllabograms may express the first sound of the logogram, or the last, or both together, or even the entire phonetic equivalent of the word. And, given the Maya writing system, they may even substitute for the logogram itself. Here are some examples:

 wi-WITZ *witz* "hill"

 BAHLAM-m(a) *bahlam* "jaguar"

 **ka-KAN** *kan* "snake"

 wi-WINIK-k(i) *winik* "man, human"

PAKAL-l(a) *pakal* "shield"

 TUUN-n(i) *tuun* "stone"

Syllabograms appear with logograms not only to hint at their reading, but also to express grammar. Those of you familiar with the Japanese script know that their own syllabograms, called *kana*, are added to logograms of Chinese origin (*kanji*) to write the grammatical suffixes to word roots. The Maya scribes did the same thing, as shall be seen in **Chapters 4** and **8,** when we examine various action (verbal) glyphs. Just to add to the complexity, there are also morphosyllables for some important suffixes; and logograms for a few plural endings.

2.5 Polyvalence

What gives the Maya script some of its flexibility, beyond the switching back and forth between logographic and syllabic signs, is **polyvalence**, a word that means "multiple values." Some signs can have more than one meaning and sound, such as a single glyph which can stand for the syllable **ku,**

and a logogram which can be read as **TUUN** (meaning "stone"). Luckily for us, though, this kind of polyvalence is rare, and when it does occur, the appropriate reading is revealed by the context. In the case of **TUUN,** the correct reading is indicated by the addition of or a -n(i) postfix (as

above). The beginning student should also be aware that a few syllabic signs can also function as logograms, such as **u** (**u-,** 3rd-person-singular Set A pronoun, "his/her/its"), **ti** (**ti-,** "at," "in," "with," "for"), and **ni** (**NI-,** "my").

Far more commonly, a single phonetic syllable or "pure" vowel will have more than one, and sometimes many, corresponding glyphs. The choice of which one to select was up to the scribe. For example, a glance at the syllabic grid will show that the sound *u* can be written by one of a number of signs – but the first given in the box, the **u**-"bracket," is by far the most frequent; it is also the one given by Landa in his "alphabet."

2.6 Conflation

Aesthetic considerations played a large role in deciding how and what a scribe wrote, and it was sometimes advisable to compress or **conflate** two discrete signs into a single glyph (*ill.* 7). A well-known case of this is the month-sign *Mol* – from ancient times this was written phonetically rather than logographically, the scribes adopting the spelling **mo-l(o)**. But it was aesthetically unacceptable to the scribes to put two signs side-by-side where a single calendrical sign should be, so they conflated these, leaving the **mo** dotted-circle to contain the **lo** syllabogram within it.

A more complex case of conflation can be seen in the variant ways the phrase *chum tuun*, "seating of the *tuun*" (a calendrical expression) could be spelled in the inscriptions. Numbers 1 and 2 below are **CHUM-m(u)-TUUN-n(i)**:

   CHUM-TUUN-n(i)

2.7 Some grammar

Even though small Maya children have no problem in learning them, the Mayan languages as they are spoken today appear forbiddingly complex and alien to us. The reader should take heart, however, from the good news that only a small part of this complexity is present in the texts, which all record the ancient literary language: the Classic Mayan tongue. Yet, as the decipherment reaches new heights of precision, it is important to know at least a modicum of Classic Mayan grammar. All those little squiggles stuck onto the "main signs" actually mean something.

Classic Mayan, like other Mayan languages, is **inflected** to express grammatical changes; inflection is largely carried out by prefixes and suffixes added to word roots, not by the kind of internal changes that appear in English (e.g. *run/ran*, *goose/geese*). Unlike German or any of the Romance languages that we may have been taught in school, there is no gender to worry about:

no intrinsically masculine, feminine, or neuter words, and no distinction between "he," "she," or "it."

Far more important to Mayan speakers is the distinction between **transitive** and **intransitive** verbs. Transitive verbs are those having both a subject and an object (English "I hit him"). Intransitives have a subject but no object ("I slept").

In English, the word order of transitive statements is generally subject-verb-object (SVO) as in the above example; in Classic Mayan it is verb-object-subject (VOS). For intransitive statements, it is verb-subject (VS), there being no object (patient). "Verb first" is the rule. Accordingly, the first glyph to occur in an ancient text after a calendrical date is the verb. We shall see in **2.7.3** that transitives take completely different pronouns from intransitives.

Adjectives always stand *before* the noun that they modify.

2.7.1 *Nouns*

There are two kinds of noun stems in Classic Mayan, "possessed" and "unpossessed" (also called "absolute"). Unpossessed nouns cannot be inflected unless a special suffix is added. Here is an example of an unpossessed stem:

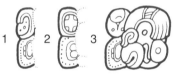

K'UH *k'uh* "god, holy"

"Possessed" stems are prefixed by a possessive (Set A) pronoun (see **2.7.3**). Some of these stems or roots take the suffix *-Vl* (vowel followed by *l*, as in *-il*, *-al*, etc.) when possessed, others do not. An example of the suffix *-il*:

u-K'UH-IL *u-k'uh-il* "his god, his holy thing"

As in the above, *-il* is usually spelled with the morphosyllabic sign **IL**, and apart from its presence with possessed nouns, it is often used to derive nouns from verb roots. In fact, it is one of the most common endings for nouns in Classic Mayan texts.

Another important *-Vl* noun suffix is *-el* (written **-EL**), attached to certain terms for statuses into which a person might be initiated, such as **AJAW-EL**, *ajaw-el*, "the status of being king" (a very prevalent phrase in sentences describing the inauguration of a ruler).

Finally, the suffix -aj (written morphosyllabically with -**AJ**) marks the unpossessed form of a class of nouns associated with things worn by humans, such as jewelry and other costume items; the most famous example concerns the jade earspools worn by the Maya elite, called *tuup*. Here it is in two forms, one unpossessed and the other possessed:

tu-pa-AJ *tuup-aj* "it is an earspool" (a stative sentence)

u-tu-p(a) *u-tuup* "it is his/her/its earspool"

What about plurals? Although the plural suffix *-oob* is ubiquitous in everyday Mayan speech, and in Colonial texts, it seems to be nearly non-existent in the Classic inscriptions. The only fully attested plural suffix is *-taak*, restricted to the plural of persons only, and of very rare occurrence. It may be spelled **ta-k(i)**, **TAAK-k(i)**, or **TAAK**. So there is no need to worry about plurals.

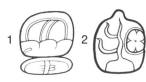

1 **ta-k(i)** *-taak* "(plural persons)"
2 **TAAK** *-taak* "(plural persons)"

2.7.2 Gender

We have said that gender really doesn't exist in any of the Mayan languages, but strictly speaking this is true only of pronouns and verbs. Actually, there is a class of nouns called **agentive**. These describe the occupation, office, or what David Stuart calls the "intrinsic quality" of a person. They are marked by prefix *Aj-* (**AJ-**) in the case of males and *Ix-* (**IX-**) for females. The sign for *Aj-* is usually the barlike syllabogram *a*, here used as a logogram, but it may also be one of the other ones on the chart (see pages 157–160). The scribes always wrote *Ix-* with a human female head distinguished by a long sinuous sidelock, a crosshatched forelock, or a motif shaped like the letters I L. It should be noted that *Aj-* may also be used by females, but always preceded by *Ix-*.

There are pages of agentive nouns in the 16th-century Motul Dictionary of Yukatek Maya, and these give a rich picture of Maya society on the eve of the Conquest. You will encounter them for both sexes throughout the Classic inscriptions. The female ones are more likely to be the personal names of queens and other royalty. Here are a few:

 AJ-tz'ib(i) *aj-tzib* "he of the writing," "scribe"

 IX-BAAK-AL-AJAW *ix-baakal-ajaw* "the queen of Palenque"
ix ajaw, "queen"
baakal, the name of the Palenque polity

2.7.3 *Pronouns*

The overwhelming majority of pronouns attached to nouns and verbs in Classic inscriptions are in the 3rd person singular ("he, she, it," "his, hers, its"). Even the use of the 1st person is rare, as are plural pronouns of any sort; the 2nd person is virtually non-existent. These were official, rigidly codified texts, probably as different from everyday Maya discourse as the modern U.S. Tax Code is from American English.

It will be remembered from **1.3** that all Mayan languages have two completely different pronoun sets. Set A goes with transitives, and Set B with intransitives; Set A is used both for the subject of transitive verbs *and* for the possessors of nouns. This state of affairs, called ergativity by linguists, is also found in Classic Mayan. Here is how the system works in Classic texts:

1) *Set A pronouns.* These are used with both nouns and verbs, and are the most common in the inscriptions; although, again, it is the 3rd person singular that is ubiquitous, and the 2nd person that is, as far as we can tell, almost totally absent except on some pottery texts.

	Singular	*Plural*
1st person	*ni-*	*ka-/kaw*
2nd person	*a-/aw-*	*i/iw-*
3rd person	*u-/(u)y-*	*u-(u)y-...-ob*

Examples:

u-tu-p(a) *u-tuup* "his earspool"

u-pi-b(i)-NAAH-IL *u-pibnaahil* "his sweatbath"

Before stems which begin with a vowel rather than a consonant, the glide consonants /y/ and /w/ serve to represent the 3rd-person-singular possessive *u*, which is then dropped. The syllabogram which is used adds the /y/ to the vowel of the stem. Examples (remember, letters in parentheses are *not* pronounced):

ya: **ya-AL-l(a)** *(u)ya-l* "her mother's child"

ye: **ye-be-t(a)** *(u)y-ebeet* "his messenger"

yi: **yi-tz'i-n(i)** *(u)y-itz'in* "his/her younger brother"

yo: **yo-OTOOT-t(i)** *(u)y-otoot* "his/her home"

yu: **yu-ne** *(u)y-une(n)* "his father's child"

2) Set B pronouns. These are suffixed to noun roots to express something about someone or something; they also appear as suffixes for intransitive verb roots to express the subject. In the following table, *ø* stands for "null," meaning that *nothing* appears in this position.

	Singular	*Plural*
1st person	*-en*	*-on*
2nd person	*-et*	*-ox*
3rd person	*-ø*	*-ob*

Since the voice of most texts is 3rd person singular, the above suffixes are mostly invisible in the glyphs and thus can be ignored by the neophyte reader.

In Classic Mayan, nouns and possessed nouns standing by themselves can be complete sentences, a concept foreign to us but understandable when one remembers that the 3rd-person-singular Set B pronoun is theoretically there, but silent:

 BAAK-k(i) *baak(-ø)* "he is a prisoner"

One can also gather from such examples that the dividing line between nouns and verbs is not very clearcut in the Mayan languages.

2.7.4 *Adjectives*

Adjectives attach directly to the front of the noun, and directly after the Set A pronoun (when this is present). They can be derived from nouns by adding a *-Vl* (*-al, -ul,* etc.) suffix, the V (vowel) usually following the Rule of Synharmony:

 ti-K'AK'-AL ju-l(u) *ti k'ak'-al jul* "with a fiery spear" *(ill. 1)*

ti, "with"

k'ak', "fire"

jul, "spear"

In the script, color terms (e.g. *chak,* "red," or *yax,* "blue-green") almost never use this suffix.

2.7.5 *Verbs*

Remember, these will appear immediately after dates. Basically, there are two kinds of verbs: **transitive** (taking an object as well as a subject) and **intransitive** (taking a subject but no object). In Classic Mayan, intransitives can be derived from transitives, and vice versa – a situation similar to that of nouns and verbs, which can also be derived from each other. Included in the category of intransitive verbs are **passive** forms, in which the subject of the verb is acted upon by somebody or by something else; passive expressions are exceedingly frequent, and are found throughout the historical texts. In the passive voice, the subject is affected by the action represented by the verb. In English, the passive often requires the auxiliary verb "to be" (e.g. "I am promoted," "he was run over"), but in Classic Mayan, the passive is carried out for one class of verbs by adding a special suffix to the verb root.

Also keep in mind that the pronoun subjects for transitive verbs are Set A, just as with possessed nouns (the pronoun is usually *u-*, the 3rd person singular), and for intransitives Set B (almost always no sound, and therefore not expressed in writing).

In the inscriptions, the only tenses that the beginning student need worry about are the past, present, and future (this last is rare). Even in historical texts talking about events earlier than the carving of a particular monument, most statements seem to be in the present. This need not seem strange to us, since history may also be written this way in English. Consider these statements:

> It is the 16th of April in the year 1789. General Washington is notified that he is elected President of the United States. Two weeks later he is inaugurated in New York.

Important note: the presence of the syllabogram 〰 -ya as a final verb suffix is a giveaway that this verb probably is in the past tense. This will be explained further in the sections which follow.

2.7.5.1 *Intransitive verbs*

Since intransitives greatly outnumber transitive verbs in the texts, we shall consider them first. Tenses are indicated by suffixes attached to the roots:

Present	Past (perfective)	Future
no suffix	*-iiy*	*-oom*

So, if there is no sign suffix at the end of an intransitive verb, it is in the present tense. If there is a 〰 -ya, indicating a final *y*, it is in the past. The example of the so-called "date indicator" (**3.5**), a word based on the root *uut*, "to happen," will illustrate these distinctions:

u-ti   *uut-i*   "it happens"   (Posterior Date Indicator)

u-ti-y(a)   *uut-iiy*   "it happened"   (Anterior Date Indicator)

u-to-m(a)   *uut-oom*   "it will happen"

You will often encounter the **-AJ** morphosyllabic sign following verb roots. Its function is to turn is to turn transitive roots into intransitive verbs, especially passive ones.

chu-k(a)-AJ   *chuhk-aj*   "he is captured"

Incidentally, this was one of the first verbs to be recognized by Knorosov, and is very common on monuments celebrating conquest. If you see someone who looks like a prisoner on a bas-relief, look for this verb immediately after a date. The personal name of the unfortunate prisoner will then follow the verb. Note that the inserted h consonant, a feature of passive verbs, is not represented in the glyphic spelling and must be reconstructed. In the past tense, a typical "capture" expression might read:

chu-ku-ji-y(a)   *chukjiiy*   "he was captured"

Another form of passive takes the suffix *-yi*. These are particularly applicable to transitive roots where things seem to happen of their own accord.

pu-lu-yi   *puluy*   "it burns"

2.7.5.2 *Positionals*

In every language of the Mayan family, there is an enormous special class of verbs that describe the position in space of the subject, such as seated, standing, prone, hanging, and so forth. In Classic Maya inscriptions, these **positionals** are largely limited to intransitives in the present or past tense, and take the suffix -*wan*, followed by a Set B pronoun (again, generally unwritten since such verbs are almost always in the 3rd person singular). They take the same tense endings as other intransitive verbs. An example of a -*wan* positional often found in texts dealing with enthronement of a king is:

 CHUM-wa-n(i) *chum-wan* "he sits"

A positional ending used for antipassives (otherwise transitive verbs that have subjects but no objects, e.g. English "he strikes") is -*laj*, expressed by either of these suffixed glyphs:

 or

2.7.5.3 *Transitive verbs*

Full transitive verbs are some of the easiest to spot in the inscriptions. They take a Set A pronoun as a prefix, usually 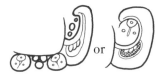 *u-*, together with a Set B suffix, always represented by the morphosyllable ⬭⬭ -*aw*. These two signs bracket the verb root to give transitives their distinctive appearance. The following example is an accession event in which a new ruler takes a scepter in the form of the god K'awiil (being transitive, the name of the subject always follows):

u-CH'AM-AW K'AWIIL *uch'am-aw* "he takes K'awiil"

Another class of transitive verbs head "secondary clauses." These follow directly after phrases in the passive voice and their function is to name the missing subject of the preceding action.

 **u-la-ji-ya** *ula-jiiy* "it was being said by"

2.8 Locative prepositions

It was important to the ancient Maya to place actions and activities in definite locations. In the inscriptions and codices, by far the most frequent locative glyph is or the syllable **ti**, first recognized in Landa's description of the Maya script. When this sign – which can also act as the syllabogram **ti** – is placed before nouns, it can have more than one meaning, though: it may stand for "to," "in," "on," "at," "as," and "for," depending on the context:

 ti CHAN *ti chan* "in heaven"

 ti 7 BEN *ti uuk 'Ben'* "on 7 Ben"

Less often, one sees the preposition **ta** 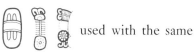 used with the same sense.

 5-ta-AJAW *ta ho Ajaw* "on 5 Ajaw"

The glyph prefix **tu** expresses an elision of the locative *ti* with the sign that follows it, the 3rd-person-singular pronoun *u*, as in:

tu-ba-hi *tu baah* "on his head"

Names of places ("toponyms", see **5.2**) may take the locative suffix -*nal*, as in these examples from the facade of the so-called Popol Nah at Copan:

Believed by some to be located around the Copan valley, they have not yet been completely deciphered.

3

TIME AND THE CALENDAR

3.1 General remarks

Almost all statements in the ancient Maya script begin with a date. The Maya were concerned not only with *where* an event took place, but *when*. Even in the codices, although it is not always immediately obvious, every action by the gods portrayed there, and even possessed nouns, are placed in the context of the complex Maya calendar. In the case of the stone monuments, there is often a whole array of dates, all interconnected by **Distance Numbers** (see **3.5**), some of them retrospective, and some of them in the present. Because of the rules of word order in Classic Mayan, in which the verb comes first, you may expect to find a verb glyph or glyphs immediately following such a date, and then (in a *transitive* statement) the object and the subject; in *intransitive* statements, the subject alone will follow the verb, and there will be no object. Knowledge of how the calendar works, and a familiarity with its glyphs, will thus help you in reading Classic inscribed texts.

Many of these dates were astronomically important: the ancient Maya had a deep knowledge of naked-eye astronomy, and the movements of the visible planets and of the sun and the moon. But they were also astrologers, and there were obviously auspicious times in which to carry out rituals, as well as times to be avoided. In particular, the astronomer/scribes took special care with the moon, eclipse dates being particularly unlucky; this is probably the reason for the elaborate **Lunar Series** (pages 51–53) that appears with the **Initial Series** (**3.4.1**) on major stelae and other monuments.

In times past, the beginning student was faced with learning a considerable amount of Maya arithmetic, and with forbidding tables, in order to calculate Maya dates. However, with the advent of hand-held calculators and with readily available computer software expressly designed for the Maya calendar, such computations may be carried out with amazing speed. A guide to these programs is to be found on page 168.

Maya time is completely cyclical: it consists of the permutations of a number of time cycles of various lengths, from the **260-day Count** (see **3.3.1**) all the way up to cycles lasting millions of years. We have cyclical time, too, most notably the eternally repeating cycle of the seven-day week, but we also have linear time, above all in the way that we count years backwards and forwards from the traditional birth date of Jesus Christ.

3.2 Maya numbers

The Maya system of numeration is amazingly economical, since it basically operates with only three digits: a dot standing for "one," a bar 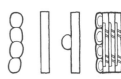 for "five," and a variable symbol for "zero" or "completion":

Thus, "four" is expressed by four dots, but "five" by a bar only, and "six" by a bar with a dot next to it. A "nineteen" consists of three bars and four dots.

For higher numbers, they used positional, base-20 notation, with the lowest to highest positions placed vertically, rather than the right-to-left, horizontal decimal scheme which we follow. But since these arithmetical calculations of higher numbers are found only in the multiplication tables and astronomical pages of the Dresden Codex, we may ignore them in this book – the highest numerical coefficient you are likely to find in the Maya monuments is the number 19.

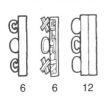

6   6   12

For aesthetic reasons, the Classic scribal sculptors did not like to leave spaces when there were only one or two dots attached to the bars (in numbers like 6 or 12), so they filled these spaces on either side of them with short, curved elements. The beginning student can be misled into thinking these fillers to be number dots, which they are not.

While the numbers 0 through 19 can be written with only the three symbols described above, for the Initial Series dates of truly grand monuments the Maya scribes and sculptors often substituted the heads of specific gods who were patrons of each number, or even full figures of those deities; the latter are usually elaborately intertwined with figures symbolizing the calendrical cycles that they modify. The finest of such stelae were carved at Quiriguá.

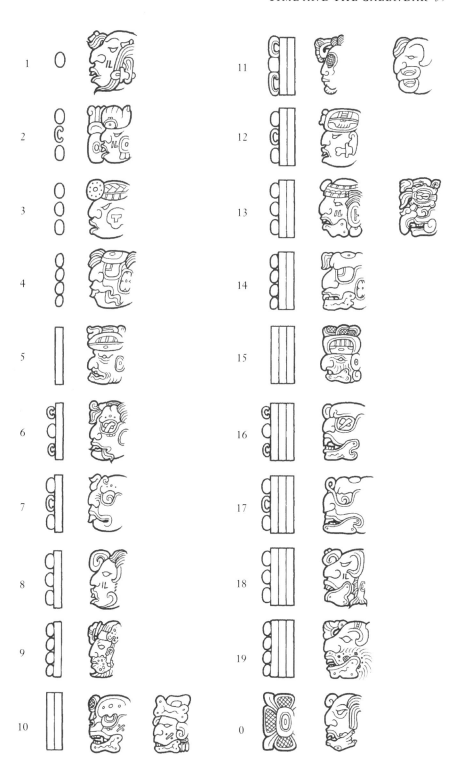

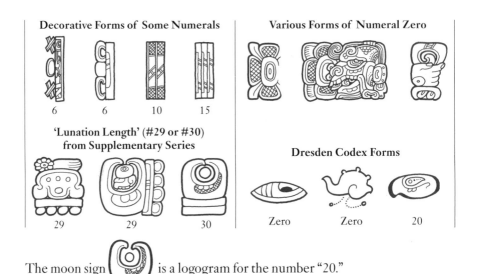

Decorative Forms of Some Numerals	Various Forms of Numeral Zero
6 6 10 15	

'Lunation Length' (#29 or #30)
from Supplementary Series

Dresden Codex Forms

29   29   30

Zero   Zero   20

The moon sign is a logogram for the number "20."

3.3 The Calendar Round

The basic part of the Maya calendar is the **Calendar Round**, an ever-repeating cycle of 52 years of exactly 365 days each. This is probably the oldest way of writing dates, since the Calendar Round was used by not only the Maya, but by all other peoples in Mesoamerica, including the Aztecs. In Maya inscriptions, it *always* follows **Long Count** dates (see **3.4**) and **Distance Numbers** (3.5). The Calendar Round is expressed by 1) a day in the **260-day Count**, with its coefficient, and 2) a month in the **Haab** or 365-day "year," with *its* coefficient. The day-sign can usually be recognized by the "cartouche" which surrounds it (an oval border, frequently with curls resembling the -*ya* syllabic sign at the bottom), although this is not always present, and is missing in the codices; and by the presence of a numerical coefficient immediately to the left or above the glyph. Here is an example of a Calendar Round date from Stela 12 at Yaxchilan:

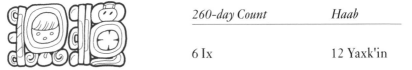

260-day Count	Haab
6 Ix	12 Yaxk'in

This date will recur every 18,980 days (52 Haabs, or 52x365), or just under 52 years.

3.3.1 *The 260-day Count*

The first part of a Calendar Round is the 260-day Count, often called in the literature by the ersatz Maya name "tzolk'in." This is also an eternally repeating cycle, and consists of the numbers 1 through 13, permutating against a

20 day signs

The 20 day signs (*ill. 3*), which always begin with Imix and end with Ajaw, are:

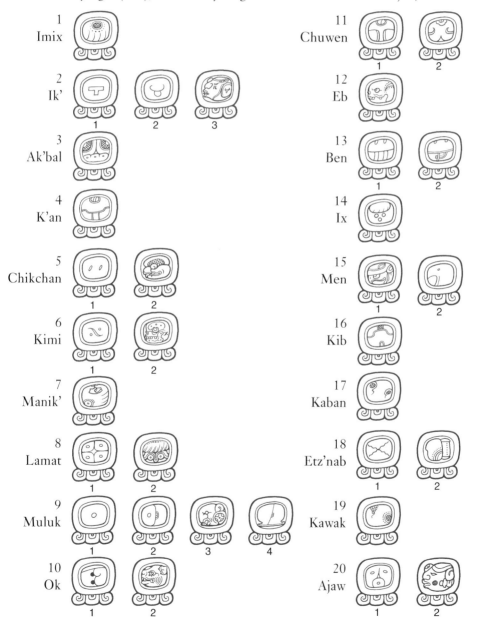

Some fancy day signs

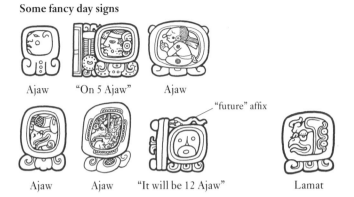

Ajaw   "On 5 Ajaw"   Ajaw

"future" affix

Ajaw   Ajaw   "It will be 12 Ajaw"   Lamat

minicycle of 20 named days. Since 13 and 20 have no common denominator, a particular day name will not recur with a particular coefficient until 260 days have passed. No one knows exactly when this extremely sacred calendar was invented, but it was certainly already ancient by the time the Classic period began. There are still highland Maya calendar priests who can calculate the day in the 260-day Count, and it is apparent that this basic way of time-reckoning has never slipped a day since its inception.

3.3.2 *The Haab*

The Haab or 365-day "year" is sometimes called the "Vague Year," since although the ancient calendar specialists were fully aware that the actual length of the year was about 365 ¼ days, they never intercalated leap days as we do, or anything similar. The Haab is also a cycle in its own right, made up of 18 months of 20 days each; because 18 x 20 is only 360 days, they added an extra "month" (the *Wayeb*) of 5 days at the end of the final full month. The coefficients 1–19 appear as the numbered day within each month. Why isn't there a "20" coefficient? Because the last or 20th day of a particular month (or 5th day of Wayeb) is called the "seating" of the *following* one, the prefix used is not a numerical coefficient, but the positional "seating" glyph, read *chum*. Thus, the "seating of Muwan" is actually the final day of K'ank'in, to be followed by 1 Muwan. Example:

 chum-muwan "seating of Muwan" (the 15th month)

By convention, however, the seating glyph is transcribed as "0" (zero).

The names that Maya specialists use for the months are all taken from the Yukatek list given to us by Bishop Landa, but it is certain that (with some exceptions) they are *not* the names as they would have been in Classic Mayan. Nevertheless, for the sake of simplicity we shall continue to use the Yukatek names:

Maya month signs

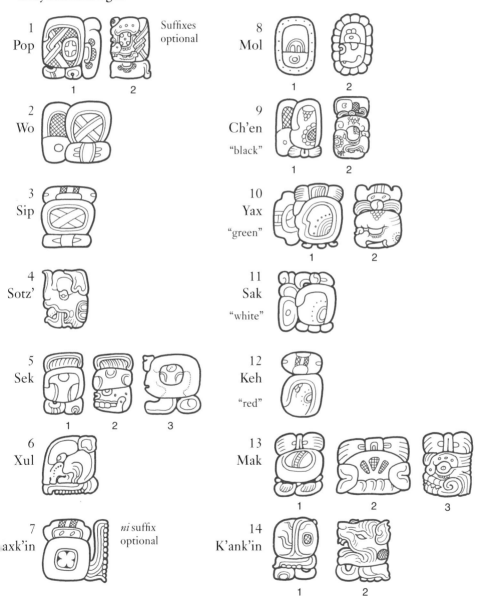

Maya month signs *continued*

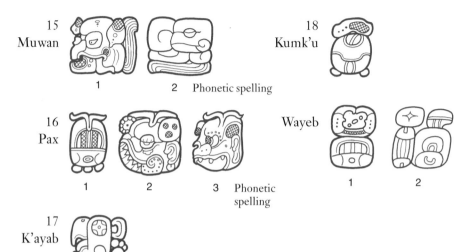

As we have seen, the Haab permutates with the 260-day Count to produce the Calendar Round (*ill. 4*). Because of the way the system operates mathematically, only certain month coefficients can occur with particular day signs of the 260-day Count, within the Calendar Round, as follows:

Day sign	*Permissible month coefficients*
Kaban, Ik', Manik', Eb	"0" (seating of month), 5, 10, 15
Etz'nab, Ak'bal, Lamat, Ben	1, 6, 11, 16
Kawak, K'an, Muluk, Ix	2, 7, 12, 17
Ajaw, Chikchan, Ok, Men	3, 8, 13, 18
Imix, Kimi, Chuwen, Kib	4, 9, 14, 19

If, in calculating the Haab for a Long Count date, you come up with an impossible month coefficient, either you or the scribe have made a mistake (it is more likely to be you!).

Immediately following the Long Count in the **Initial Series** (see **3.4.1**) is the position in the 260-day Count, but this is usually separated from the Haab and its coefficient by lunar notations and other glyphs that shall be considered below.

EXERCISE 2

Transcribe the following Calendar Round glyphs:

Answers on page 169

3.4 The Long Count and the Initial Series

If the Maya reckoned important dates, such as the accession of a king, only by the Calendar Round, there would be considerable confusion over exactly when this event took place, for the same Calendar Round date will occur every 52 "years" or Haabs. The Maya avoided this ambiguity by the simultaneous use of the **Long Count**, a count of days elapsed since the starting point of the Long Count calendar on 8 September 3114 BC, according to the most accepted correlation of the Maya and Christian calendars. The Long Count itself is a gigantic permutation calendar, with the possibility of calculating millions of years into the past and the future. It consists of cycles of various magnitudes, each with its numerical coefficient by which it is to be multiplied; all of the products of these operations are to be added together, and the days counted forward from the mythical starting point. These cycles with their magnitudes are as follows:

"Bak'tun"	20 k'atuns or 144,000 days
K'atun	20 tuns or 7,200 days
Tun	18 winals or 360 days
Winal	20 k'ins or 20 days
K'in	1 day

It is by no means certain that these names, which are in Yukatek, are exactly

Ordinary period glyphs

	Simple, abstract forms	*Head-variants*	*Full-figure glyphs*	
			Copan Stela I	Yaxchilan Lintel 48	Palenque Palace Tablet
"Bak'tun" 20 k'atuns/ 144,000 days	Phonetic pi-h(i) = "bundle"	"Bird with hand-jaw"		
K'atun 20 tuns/ 7,200 days		"Bird"		
Tun 18 winals/ 360 days	"Drum"	"Skull-Jaguar-Bird"	"Lilypad Serpent"	

what a speaker and writer of Classic Mayan would have called them, with the exception of "k'in." The word "bak'tun," for example, is an invention of late 19th-century epigraphers. The "tun" was surely called *haab*, but in order not to confuse it with the 365-day year, we will continue to use the traditional term.

There exist higher cycles on a few monuments, but these five are the ones that occur in most date inscriptions. Each Long Count cycle has its own hieroglyph, which may be simple or may be a more elaborate head or even full-figure variant depicting the god ruling over that cycle:

Immediately to the left of each cycle is the number (in bar-and-dot or more elaborate form) of its coefficient; these are conventionally written in the Mayanist literature with Arabic numerals (from 0 to 19), with each cycle

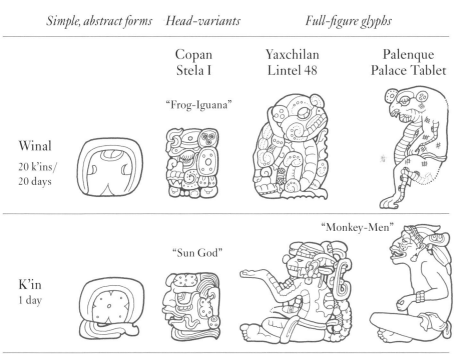

	Simple, abstract forms	*Head-variants*	*Full-figure glyphs*
		Copan Stela I	Yaxchilan Lintel 48	Palenque Palace Tablet
Winal 20 k'ins/ 20 days		"Frog-Iguana"		
K'in 1 day		"Sun God"		"Monkey-Men"

position separated from its neighbors by a dot. So, a Long Count notation of 9.14.0.10.6 would mean "9 bak'tuns plus 14 k'atuns plus 0 tuns plus 10 winals plus 6 k'ins," or 1,397,006 days since the inception of the Long Count.

Any position in the Long Count is also a position in the Calendar Round, and therefore in Classic texts a Calendar Round date always follows a Long Count date. It is clear that the beginning date of the current Maya era is really

Some trans-bak'tun period glyphs

	Simple, abstract forms	*Head-variants*
"Kinchiltun" 20 kalabtuns/ 1,152,000,000 days		
"Kalabtun" 20 piktuns/ 57,600,000 days		
"Piktun" 20 bak'tuns/ 2,880,000 days		

the completion date of a preceding Maya era; this is 13.0.0.0.0, falling on a Calendar Round of 4 Ajaw 8 Kumk'u, from which all dates in the present Great Cycle are calculated. Our own Great Cycle is scheduled to end about five millennia later, on 13.0.0.0.0 4 Ajaw 3 K'ank'in or 23 December 2012 in the Gregorian calendar (10 December 2012 in the Julian calendar).

3.4.1 *The Initial Series*

On a typical Maya monument, the very first Long Count date is called the **Initial Series**, and it stands prominently in the farthest upper left of the text. Situated just above it, near the top edge, is a large glyph extending over two columns. This is the **Introductory Glyph**, which basically consists of a tun main sign flanked by a pair of fish or fish fins. No one knows exactly how it is to be read. Between these latter is a variable element, either a deity or a glyph or glyph combination standing for it; this is the patron god of the

varies according to month

month in the Haab. The Introductory Glyph is always a clue that an Initial Series follows. The Long Count of the Initial Series ends with the k'in sign and its coefficient. The very first glyph following this is the day in the 260-day Count – always an Ajaw if the k'in coefficient is a "zero."

EXERCISE 3

Transcribe this Initial Series with Calendar Round from Stela 3 at Piedras Negras. For teaching reasons, we have moved the Haab next to the day in the 260-day Count; in actuality, it appears following the Supplementary Series (see below).

Answers on page 169

3.4.2 *The Supplementary Series*

One would logically expect the Haab position (the month and its day number) to be written right after the 260-day Count, but this is almost never the case in an Initial Series: between the two are usually placed six or seven other glyphs, the so-called **Supplementary Series**. Early epigraphers recognized that the glyphs at the end of this series were much more consistent than those at the beginning, so they labeled them in reverse order: G, F, E, D, C, B, A. Later scholars discerned additional elements within the sequence which had been missed by the first decipherers, and named them Z, Y, and X. This cumbersome situation seems specifically designed to confuse the neophyte, but do not be daunted: it confuses even experienced epigraphers. In the interest of simplicity, we shall discuss only the most common of these, and skip Y, Z, and the rest. The reader is directed to Thompson (1971) and to Harris and Stearns (1997) for a more detailed treatment of these.

The easiest part to deal with consists of **Glyph G** and its modifier **Glyph F**, which occur right after the day sign of the 260-day Count. Glyph G is actually a never-ending cycle of 9 gods (labeled G1, G2, G3…), similar to the Nine Lords of the Night among the Aztecs; since 360 is divisible by 9 with no remainder, G9 always falls at the end (or completion) of the tun, k'atun, and bak'tun cycles, i.e. when their coefficients are "zero." G9 is clearly the aged god of darkness, the Night Sun, but the others have not yet been convincingly identified.

Glyph F is still undeciphered, reading *?-huun*, having something to do with books, paper, or headdresses (all pronounced *huun*). Its widely varied spellings provided epigraphers with the evidence for the equivalence of the "knot," "Jester God," "codex," and other glyphs.

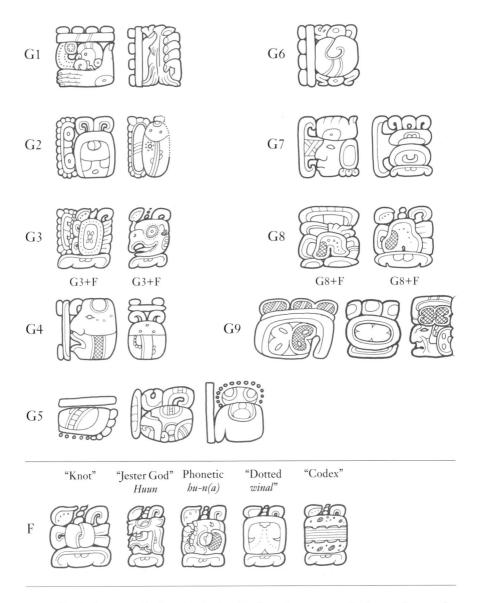

| "Knot" | "Jester God" Huun | Phonetic hu-n(a) | "Dotted winal" | "Codex" |

All of the rest of the glyphs in the Supplementary Series make up the **Lunar Series** (see *opposite*). This is a complex topic which we will deal with only briefly here. Basically this is what these glyphs tell us:

- How many days have elapsed since the last New Moon.
- The position of a particular lunar month (lunation) in a cycle of six lunations (about 177 days).
- Whether the current lunar month has 29 or 30 days.

THE LUNAR SERIES

The Maya were deeply concerned with the state of the moon on a particular date, since that determined whether or not a solar or lunar eclipse might occur. This was an important calculation, for in their minds such an awesome event would probably have had dire consequences. As a consequence, many of the glyphs following the Long Count date in an **Initial Series** inscription are concerned with the moon, and are to be found between the day sign and the month sign (in the **Calendar Round**). You will sometimes see these glyphs referred to as the **Lunar Series**. They are as follows, in the order of their appearance (but bear in mind that not every possible glyph in the series appears on a particular monument):

Glyphs E and D

These two express the number of days that have elapsed since the last New Moon. The average length of a "moon" or lunation is 29 ½ days, from one New Moon (when the entire moon is darkened) to the next, so the value here may never exceed 29. Glyph D represents a number attached to the root form **hu-li-ya** or **HUL-li-ya**, "it arrived." The reading of this unit is something like "23 arrived," or more loosely, "It was the 23rd day of this moon." The preceding Glyph E only appears when the value of D is 20 or higher and more space is required to give the number.

Perhaps due to the Maya scribes' love of visual puns, the E-D glyphs contain three different signs shaped like the moon, none of which actually mean "moon"! The first seems not to be read at all, it is simply part of an elaborated version of the verb **HUL** (1st example). The second serves as the numeral 20, perhaps **K'AL**, distinguished from -**ja** by its single large inner dot (2nd and 3rd examples). The third is another **HUL** logogram, with an almond-shaped "eye" replacing the inner dot (4th example).

11D (11 days arrived)

6ED (26 days arrived)

2ED (22 days arrived)

14D (14 days arrived)

10D (10 days arrived)

Glyph C

This gives the position of a particular lunation within a cycle of six lunations (6 x 29.5 =177 days). The coefficients therefore vary from 1 to 6. The glyph can be recognized by the 'flat-hand' verb suffixed by 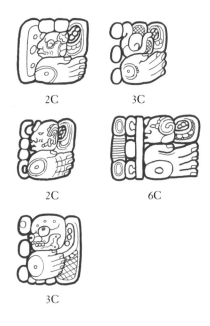 -**AJ**, surmounted by

one of three small, variable god heads. Each row of the illustration is devoted to one of these heads. Glyph C was probably important in eclipse predictions, since the ancient astronomers knew that if a lunar eclipse occurs, another one might happen 177 days later, or even several separated by the same interval.

2C   3C

2C   6C

3C

Glyph X

Glyph X modifies Glyph C, and represents the proper names or epithets of specific gods presiding over each lunation. There are six classes of Glyph X, dependent upon the coefficient of Glyph C. The specific form of Glyph X within each class has a number of variants, of which we have illustrated only the most common. Each row in our

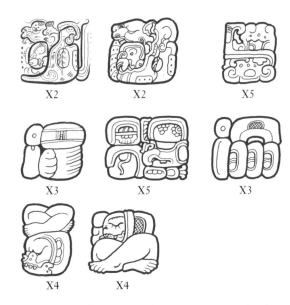

X2   X2   X5

X3   X5   X3

X4   X4

figure shows Glyph X's that correspond to the god head in the same row in the Glyph C figure above. It was long ago recognized that the influence of a god in the series begins halfway through one lunation, and continues halfway through the next. As with Glyphs E and D, as our understanding of this unfamiliar calendrical cycle has developed, designations for the various versions of this glyph (originally called X1, X2, etc.) have changed, unnecessarily complicating any explanation.

Glyph B

This is a modifier for Glyph X, and is read *u k'aba'*, "its name" (example 1), or *u ch'ok k'aba*, "its princely name" (examples 2–4).

1   2   3   4

Glyph A

Glyph A consists of the "moon-sign" read "twenty," plus the bar-and-dot numbers 9 or 10. It thus tells one whether the current lunation has 29 or 30 days. Although as we have said, the synodic lunar month is about 29 1/2 days, the Maya astronomers didn't deal in fractions but in integral or whole numbers. Therefore they calculated that the six-lunation cycle had three 29-day "moons," and three 30-day "moons."

29 days   29 days

30 days

Note: If you are interested in finding out Glyphs D/E, C, and A for a particular Long Count date, you can use the computer software programs referenced on page 168.

Why did they go to all this trouble? The ancient Maya were first-class astronomers, capable of calculating the dates of possible lunar and solar eclipses from observations like these. Eclipses were extremely ill-omened events, and it must have been important to set the events recorded by Initial Series dates so as to avoid such evil occurrences.

3.5 Distance Numbers, Period Endings, and anniversaries

It is helpful to think of the calendrical part of a Maya inscription as a kind of skeleton underlying the rest of the text, the latter being the flesh, so to speak.

The first thing to do is to figure out the skeleton. In any long monumental text, there is usually more than one date; in fact, there may be up to four, five or even more calendrical expressions, connected with each other by what are known as **Distance Numbers,** which may or may not be announced by a **Distance Number Introductory Glyph.** The usual form of this shows the 3rd-person possessive pronoun *u-* at the top or to the left of the logogram for the verb *tz'ak,* "to set in order," over the morphosyllabic sign for -*aj,* as below:

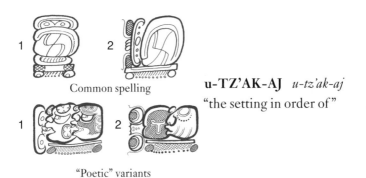

Common spelling

u-TZ'AK-AJ *u-tz'ak-aj*
"the setting in order of"

"Poetic" variants

Like Initial Series dates, Distance Numbers are written in the Long Count system, *but in reverse order:* the k'in number is given first (without the cycle sign, or with a shell-like substitute),  then the winals, followed by the tuns, and so forth. The Distance Number count

may be either forward or backward from the last date given in the text, according to which of two alternative expressions is found just after the Distance Number:

i-u-t(i) *i-uut* "and then it happens"
(that is, count forward to…)

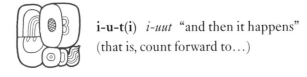

u-t(i)-y(a) *uutiiy* "it happened"
(count backward to…)

The best way to distinguish these two is to look for 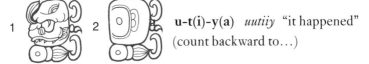, the syllabic **i-** prefix in the former, and, the syllabic **-ya** suffix in the latter. By moving forward or backward, one arrives at another date, which is always given as a Calendar Round only, although the new Long Count position is implied. Here is an example taken from Lintel 21 at Yaxchilan:

5 k'ins, 16 winals, 1 tun,

15 k'atuns, and then it happens

(on) 7 Muluk 17 Sek (the Calendar Round)

In other words, one is to count forward 108,365 days (almost 297 years) from the previous date given on the lintel, which is the Initial Series date 9.0.19.2.4 2 K'an 2 Yax. By doing this, one does in fact reach 9.16.1.0.9 7 Muluk 17 Sek, a day on which the current Yaxchilan ruler, the famous "Bird Jaguar," dedicated a building.

EXERCISE 4

Transcribe and translate this short text taken from Stela 12 at Piedras Negras.

Answers on page 169

The Maya were particularly interested in positions in the Long Count calendar marked by the completion of major cycles within it, above all the ending of bak'tuns and k'atuns. Within the k'atuns, it would be the completion of 5, 10, and 15 tuns. In our modern way of writing Long Count numbers, such "red letter" dates might be 9.12.0.0.0, or 9.15.5.0.0. Such **Period Endings** are often indicated by , a sign like a horizontal hand with a flower-like element hanging from the tip of the index finger, known to be the logogram for *tzutz*, "to end"; this is one of a large class of intransitive verbs that takes a synharmonic *-Vl* suffix followed by *-y*. Here it is always in the present:

TZUTZ-(u)-y(i) HOLAHUN (k'atun)
tzutz-uy holajuun (k'atun) "it ends, the 15th k'atun"

Note: the exact reading of the k'atun sign in Classic Mayan remains unknown (see **3.3**).

There were other ways of indicating Period Endings, but this is a subject beyond the scope of this brief manual. Period Endings always fall on the day Ajaw, so that if there is an Ajaw in a Calendar Round not directly associated with an Long Count date, one should suspect that this *is* a Period Ending. Long Count **anniversaries** of important events in the life of a ruler, such as his birth-date, were also occasionally written on Maya monuments, sometimes as the completion of one or more k'atuns, using the same pointing-hand sign (**TZUTZ**) as in Period Endings.

Half-periods, that is, the completion of 10 tuns or 10 k'atuns, may be marked with a special glyph:

TAN-LAM *tan-lam* "half-diminished"

The beginning student should learn how to recognize and read such dates and their associated glyphs, even if he or she is not prepared to work out all of the calendrical mathematics. There are some compelling reasons for this: 1) calen-drical expressions, whether brief or extensive, are almost always immediately followed by the action which took place on that day, and the names and titles of the principal actors; 2) once one has identified all the calendrical glyphs, what remains is the heart of the text – to many of us, this is the really interesting part. This holds true even of the codices, in which the protagonists are gods rather than humans.

EXERCISE 5

This is the text on the upper surface of Altar Q, Copan. To test your knowledge of the Maya calendar, write out the Calendar Rounds and Distance Numbers. If you have access to one of the software programs listed on page 168, give the Long Count positions of each Calendar Round (it is known that the first Calendar Round on the altar corresponds to 8.19.10.10.17).

Note: when doing Long Count arithmetic, remember that the winal coefficient can never be more than 17! Here is a model (hypothetical) of how Mayanists write out such chronologies:

9. 7. 0.16.16	5 Kib 14 Keh
+ 7.17. 5	
9. 7. 8.16. 1	10 Imix 19 Ch'en
+ 1. 1.19	
9. 7.10. 0. 0	6 Ajaw 13 Sak

Answers on page 169

EXERCISE 6

In order to test your ability to read the most commonly encountered kind of calendrical inscription, read this complete (and fairly standard) Initial Series from the left side of Piedras Negras Stela 10:

Answers on page 169

4

ROYAL LIVES AND ROYAL RITUALS

4.1 General remarks

You now understand that verbal glyphs are easy to recognize, since for the most part they immediately follow time expressions (there are a few rare reversals, in which the verb appears *before* the Calendar Round), and they are very often intransitive, taking the passive ending   -**AJ.**

Ever since Proskouriakoff first recognized birth and inauguration glyphs in the Piedras Negras inscriptions, epigraphers have steadily added to the corpus of verbs whose meanings are understood in a general way; but it has only been in recent years that most of these can be read in a Mayan language, and their grammatical endings clarified. A large part of such "action verbs" describe events in the lives of the Maya kings and their immediate families.

4.2 Life-cycle events

There are various life-cycle events and rituals that appear in the inscriptions, but the ones that play the most important roles, to the extent that they are often commemorated by later anniversaries, are birth, accession, and death.

4.2.1 *Birth*

As among other Mesoamerican cultures, the birth dates of both living rulers and supernatural ancestral deities were noted with great care (*ill. 8*). In the case of the Classic Maya, these were usually expressed as Calendar Round positions reached retrospectively by Distance Numbers that count back in time; readers were expected to mentally fill in the appropriate Long Count positions. In her landmark 1960 paper, Proskouriakoff showed that the "main sign" of the birth verb was the so-called "Upended Frog" glyph.

We now know that this stands for the logogram **SIH** followed by verbal endings (the syllabogram **hu** superficially resembles **SIH**, but lacks the series of "beads" surrounding the head). For the neophyte, it is probably the most easily recognized Maya verb, with few variations. Here are some royal birth expressions, the first following the birth date of one of Yaxchilan's greatest kings, the second that of a mighty king of Naranjo:

SIH-ya-AJ ya-YAXUUN-BAHLAM-m(a)
si(h)y-aj yaxuun-bahlam
"Yaxuun-Bahlam was born"

Note: Although many continue to use the name "Bird-Jaguar" for this king, the bird prefixing the jaguar head is the Lovely Cotinga, whom the Maya call *yaxuun.*

SIH-ya-AJ K'AK'-TILI-w(i)
CHAN-n(a)-CHAAK
si(h)y-aj k'ak'-tiliw chan chaak
"K'ak' Tiliw Chan Chaak
was born"

Vocabulary:

 K'AK *k'ak'* "fire"

 CHAN *chan* "sky, heaven"

 CHAAK-k(i) *Chaak* "Chaak" (the Rain God)

A less common glyph compound expressing birth, but still undeciphered, shows a hand over the logogram or syllabograms standing for "earth" (*kab*), preceded by the 3rd-person-singular pronoun *u*, "his" or "her":

1 **u-?-KAB** *u-?-kab*   2 **u-?-ka-b(a)** *u-?-kab*

4.2.2 *Accession*

The next really significant event in the life of a royal personage was his accession to power, sometimes after several months or even years had passed since the demise of his predecessor (presumably a regent had filled in for him). At Piedras Negras, certain stelae show the newly inaugurated king seated in a niche raised upon a scaffold, a visual clue that enabled Proskouriakoff to identify one of the most common glyphs for accession. This is the so-called "Toothache Glyph," an animal head or a moon-sign tied up with a band surmounted by a knot. It is read by some epigraphers as the logogram **HOK'**, standing for *hok'*, "knot" – apparently a reference to the tying on of a royal headband, a supreme act similar to the crowning of a European king. However, David Stuart has been positing a value of **JOY**.

1   2

Another very common accession glyph reads **CHUM**, "to be seated," that is, to be enthroned. It and a related glyph depicting the lower part of a body are positional verbs clearly indicating enthronement, and usually take positional endings (see **2.7.5.2**):

CHUM-m(u)-wa-ni *chum-wan-i* "he sits"

Usually, both the "Toothache Glyph" and the "seating" glyphs are immediately succeeded by the phrase **ti-AJAW-le(l)**, *ti ajaw-lel,* "in the kingship," then by the king's name:

CHUM-?-wa-ni ti-AJAW-le(l)
chum-wan-i ti- ajaw-lel "he sits in the kingship"
(for glyphs expressing *ajaw*, "king," see **6.1**).

4.2.3 *Death and burial*

The Maya kings (and their queens) were buried in splendor inside elaborately equipped tombs within the great pyramids, or sometimes in plaza areas in front of the pyramids, and the dates of both demise and the burial rite were sometimes recorded on monuments raised by their successors. As in our own society, the Maya scribes found ways to express the death of an individual in euphemisms, similar to our use of the phrase "he passed away." One such expression is:

 **K'A'-(a)-y(i) u-SAK-NICH?-IK'-IL**
k'a'ay u-saknich? ik'il "it ends, the white flower-wind"

 SAK *sak* "white"   **NICH?** *nich?* "flower"

 IK' *ik'* "wind"

The verb *k'a'ay* means "it ended" in Ch'orti', the daughter language of Classic Mayan, and "white flower-wind" presumably refers to the breath or soul of the departed. The **SAK** and **NICH?** signs can be conflated into a single sign. Here is another euphemistic combination that appears at Copan and on the famous Palenque sarcophagus of King Janaab Pakal:

 OCH-BIH *och bih* "he enters the road"

The "road" here is most likely the Milky Way, the path of souls on their journey to Xibalba, the land of the dead.

The date of interment was also commemorated, followed by the verbal phrase:

 mu-ka-AJ *muk-aj* "he is buried"

4.3 Ritual activities

Next to life-cycle events, the rituals celebrated by rulers (and their families) throughout their lives make up the bulk of the texts recorded on Maya monuments, and to a lesser extent on the secondary texts painted or carved on pottery vessels. Most of these have been deciphered, but there are a few rites about which we remain ignorant.

4.3.1 *Period Ending rites*

A large proportion of surviving Maya monuments, particularly from sites in the Department of the Peten, Guatemala, commemorate the completion of k'atuns, half-k'atuns (that is, 10 tuns), and hotuns (5 tuns) in the Long Count calendar. On these red-letter dates, the richly adorned ruler stands, often above a prone captive, and usually wields in his right hand the so-called "mannikin scepter"; this is an image of the snake-footed god K'awiil, a potent symbol of royal descent (see **11.3**). He may also carry the so-called "ceremonial bar," a stylized sky-serpent that probably represents the Milky Way. The glyphs tell us that upon this date a "hand-scattering" rite was held, involving the sprinkling of copal incense fragments or of some kind of liquid, probably blood, into censers or even over tombs and bones of ancestors. The verb, the root of which reads **CHOK** ('to sprinkle'), immediately follows the glyph(s) for the period completed; it may be postfixed by syllabic **ch'a-ji**, here standing for *ch'aaj*, "incense." An example from Stela 15 at Dos Pilas is:

ti-TAN-LAM-AW u-CHOK-AW-ch'a-j(i)
ti tanlam-aw u-chok-aw-ch'aaj
"at the half-period, it was incense-sprinkled"

The text then goes on to name the spot that was so honored, and the name of the ruler who carried out the rite.

The other verb associated with Period Ending rituals describes the taking up of the K'awiil scepter itself by the monarch, in a display of power. The key glyph here is a hand directed left, with upraised thumb; in the crook of the hand is a sign resembling the Ajaw day glyph.

This is a logogram read **CH'AM/K'AM**, "to take." It is followed by the truncated sign for K'awiil, a forehead device emitting smoke. Sometimes there is conflation, and the K'awiil glyph is placed in the crook. Here is such a statement (see **2.7.5.1** for the function of the -*aw* suffix):

CH'AM-AW K'AWIIL

ch'am-aw k'awiil "K'awiil gets taken"

A further royal ritual recently identified by David Stuart is the "binding of the stone," which also commemorated Period Endings, in this instance the completion of k'atuns. As suggested by Stuart, the stones – stelae and even altars – may actually have been tied up, while the ruler sprinkled

u-CHOK-ch'a-j(i) *u-chok-ch'aaj* "he incense sprinkles"

his blood on the holy monuments. The associated verb is the **TUUN** sign over a flat hand, a collocation now read as **K'AL-TUUN**, "to stone-tie," thus:

u-K'AL-AW-TUUN-ni

u-k'al-aw-tuun "his stone gets bound"

4.3.2 Bloodletting

It was an obligation of members of the royal line to ceremonially shed their own blood in honor of the gods and the deified ancestors. For males, this meant piercing one's penis with a bone awl or stingray spine; for their wives, the drawing of a thorn-spiked rope or string through the tongue (*ill. 1*). On the testimony of lintels from Yaxchilan, these painful acts conjured up what Linda

Schele called "vision serpents," with ancestors emerging from their open jaws (*ill. 2*). There are two alternative verbs expressing this bloodletting and/or conjuring event, the so-called "fish-in-hand" glyph (which may substitute for the main sign of the Glyph G1 in the Lords of the Night series), and the "lancet" glyph:

TZAK   *tzak*   "to conjure"

CH'AB   *ch'ab*   "to do penance"

4.3.3 *God impersonation*

On Classic Maya monuments, rulers are often shown masked as gods, especially deities associated with war, such as the Jaguar God of the Underworld. The associated pair of glyphs standing for this action show that they are in, in fact, *impersonating* these gods. The first member of the pair has the extremely important combination read as **u-ba-h(i)**, *u-baah*, an expression basically meaning "his/her self" or "his/her image"; *u-baah* can appear by itself in front of the names of high-ranking persons in all sorts of texts. In god-impersonation statements, it is followed by a second glyph that has not yet been deciphered:

u-ba-hi-IL...?   *u-baahil...?*   "he is the...?"

4.3.4 *Royal dance*

Music and dance probably took place during all great ceremonies and feasts, and the great lords took part in these, a custom that lasted until the Spanish Conquest. Maya artists depicted the dance of kings in subtle fashion, usually showing just one leg slightly raised and bent so that the ball of the foot barely touches the ground. In the associated texts, the action of dancing is given by the intransitive verb *ak'ta*, "to dance":

AK'-ta-AJ *ak'taj* "he dances"

4.3.5 *Ballplaying and ballcourts*

Difficult as it may be for us to conceive of a ballgame as a ritual activity, for the Classic Maya it was as much a religious as a sporting event. There are numberless representations of rulers and other noble personages playing ball in Maya art, whether on stelae or panels, or upon painted or carved vases. In these scenes, they wear the "yoke"-type padded belt and other protective gear, and the ball is frequently shown in play. The verb root "to play ball" is *pitz*, expressed by various combinations of glyph elements, but commonly introduced by the syllabogram **pi**:

pi-tz(i)-AJ *pitz-aj* "ball is played"

The royal ballplayer was given the title of *aj pitz*, thus:

AJ-pi-tz(i)

The court itself had its own glyph, a yet-undeciphered logogram showing the ball bouncing down a profile set of steps:

?-na

4.3.6 *Postscript*

The foregoing by no means represents *all* the royal rituals that find expression in the glyphs. Many more are known, and many have yet to be discovered and deciphered. But these are the ceremonial actions that you are most likely to see in Classic relief texts, following a date. In frequency, they come second only to the war glyphs to be presented in Chapter 8.

5

PLACES AND POLITIES

One of the great moments in Maya decipherment took place in 1958, when Heinrich Berlin published his groundbreaking article on **Emblem Glyphs** in a French journal. This was one of the factors that enabled Proskouriakoff to conclude in 1960 that the Classic Maya inscriptions were mainly concerned with royal dynasties and their various histories. Subsequently, through the analysis of Emblem Glyphs and their distribution over the Maya lowlands, scholars have put together a convincing political geography for the Classic city-states. These glyphs are ubiquitous on Maya monuments, and the beginning epigrapher should learn to recognize each and every one of them.

Within the past decade, David Stuart and Stephen Houston have further refined ancient Maya geopolitics through the identification of **toponyms**, proper names not only of the Maya cities, but of specific locations within them. Their study partly answers an old question first raised by Berlin: did the Emblem Glyphs also function as place names, or were they the names of the royal lineages that ruled these kingdoms? The most recent scholarship says that while they may well have begun as toponyms, in time they came to be applied to the entire territory controlled by a particular *k'uhul ajaw* ("holy king"). Nonetheless, with a few exceptions, the toponyms for cities are *not* the same as their Emblem Glyphs (see **5.2**).

A significant byproduct of the Stuart-Houston study is that we now know the actual Maya names of some of their great cities, not the often imaginative ones that have been associated with them since the Spanish Conquest (or ersatz ones dreamed up by archaeologists).

5.1 Emblem Glyphs

Emblem Glyphs usually immediately follow the personal name or names of royal personages – kings and their wives – when these appear in a sentence.

Each Emblem Glyph consists of three parts:

1   A "main sign" which varies according to the particular polity involved.

2   A prefix with dots or beads attached to another variable sign.
This sign, more fully written attached to the profile head of "God C," is actually the logogram **K'UHUL**, "holy."

3   A superfix (above the main sign), , now known to be one of the logograms for *ajaw*, "king" or "lord." In some cases the -**w(a)** syllabogram appears below or to the right of the main sign as a phonetic complement for **AJAW**. Because of its prestigious nature, the **AJAW** sign is placed above, but it is read last.

So, the entire collocation can be translated as "Holy King of _____"

 [idealized EG]

While most cities have only one Emblem Glyph, Palenque and Yaxchilan have two (often, what appear to be different Emblem Glyphs within a polity are just variants, such as the two skeletal signs within the one for Palenque). The explanation of the fact that Tik'al and Dos Pilas share Emblem Glyphs would appear to be that the Dos Pilas royal house came from Tik'al.

Emblem Glyphs of major cities of the southern lowlands

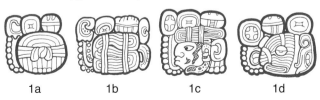

1a   1b   1c   1d

Tik'al

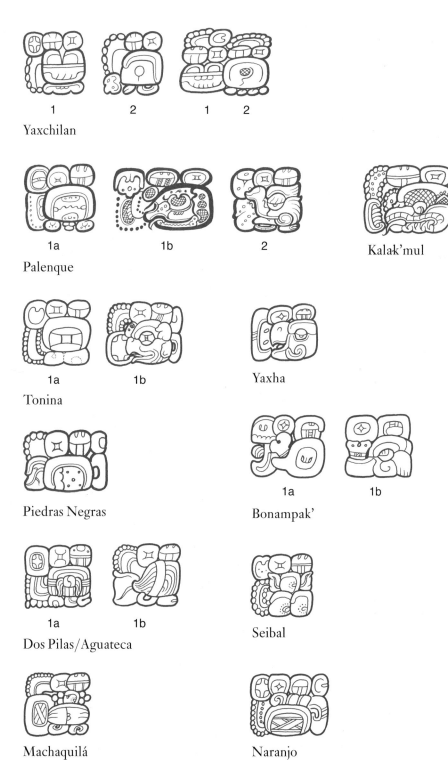

1   2   1   2
Yaxchilan

1a   1b   2   Kalak'mul
Palenque

1a   1b   Yaxha
Tonina

Piedras Negras

1a   1b
Bonampak'

1a   1b   Seibal
Dos Pilas/Aguateca

Machaquilá   Naranjo

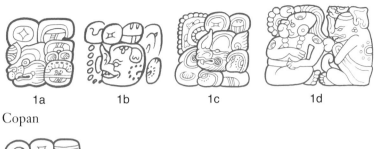

1a   1b   1c   1d

Copan

Quiriguá

5.2 Toponyms (place-names)

A frequent expression in the inscriptions is the verb *uutiiy*, "it happened"

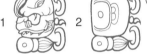

(see **3.5**), followed by one or two glyphs that Stuart

and Houston demonstrate make up a toponym or place-name. One would logically expect a locative preposition such as ⬡ **ti**, *ti*, "at" between these parts of speech, but it appears that the scribe could and often did drop this – the reader was supposed to mentally supply this. The Maya scribes were sticklers when it came to verb and noun morphology, but took shortcuts elsewhere. In all events, such a formula has led to the recognition of quite a few toponyms (described in **5.2**), including a few that are clearly supernatural places.

So, putting together information from both these and from those Emblem Glyph main signs that also seem to be toponyms, we can now know what the ancient Maya themselves called some of their greatest cities.

Maya city names

Tik'al   **MUTAL**   *Mutal*

1a   1b

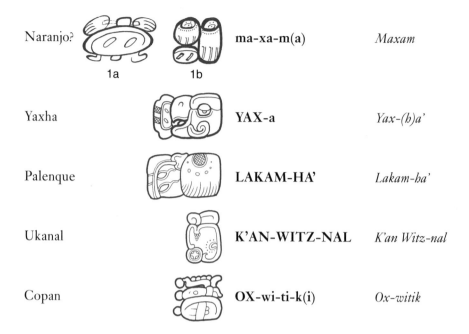

Naranjo?	1a 1b	**ma-xa-m(a)**	*Maxam*
Yaxha		**YAX-a**	*Yax-(h)a'*
Palenque		**LAKAM-HA'**	*Lakam-ha'*
Ukanal		**K'AN-WITZ-NAL**	*K'an Witz-nal*
Copan		**OX-wi-ti-k(i)**	*Ox-witik*

Comments:

Yaxha may be the only Maya city that has retained its ancient name until today. There was a major calligrapher and vase painter named Aj Maxam ("he of Maxam") at Naranjo; he was of royal blood. *Lakam-ha'* means "Great Waters," probably a reference to the streams that run down from the hills above, both through and nearby Palenque. The principal main sign of the Palenque Emblem Glyph reads **BAAK** "bone" (p. 70: 1a, b), although this dynasty also used a second: **MAT**, the name of a mythical bird (p. 70: 2).

Quite a few identified toponyms have in their names either **WITZ** (*witz*, "mountain") or **NAL** (probably meaning "place"), or both (as in the case of Ukanal), and many dynasts on the monuments stand on gigantic **WITZ** glyphs – such a ruler is literally "king of the mountain." They may also stand on their own city's toponym, written large.

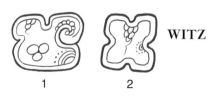

WITZ

1   2

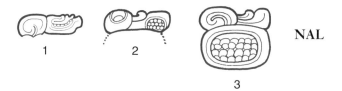

NAL

K'an Witz-nal could therefore be translated as "Yellow Mountain."

The Maya were great namers of everything – rivers, mountains, cities, buildings, architectural features, and all sorts of ritual and personal objects, as we shall see later. In everything they did and said, they took pains to place themselves not only in time but also in space.

6

DYNASTIC NAMES
AND TITLES

There is a great deal of history recorded on the Maya stone monuments. Even though we don't have long king lists like those for the Egyptian pharaohs, a surprising number of Classic Maya rulers and members of their families *are* known, at least by their hieroglyphic names, and we have a good idea of when they were born and when they died (for a complete and up-to-date listing, city by city, see Martin and Grube 2000). We are also getting a grasp on royal titles and epithets.

There are still many details to be worked out with the glyphs associated with the royal house and with subsidiary nobles. In the first place, even the readings proposed for some names and titles as recently as the 1980s are now known to be wrong (that is, the study of phonetic-syllabic combinations that occasionally substitute for logograms has proved that they were wrong). Second, we still don't know the exact functions of some of the titles (and offices) that we actually *can* read with confidence. And lastly, the personal names of many rulers were written purely with logograms – often the heads of fantastic animals – that have so far defied decipherment, since we haven't yet found any phonetic substitutions for them. Until the day when this happens, we are reduced to referring to these exalted personages by nicknames or by numbers (Ruler 1, Ruler 2, and so on).

6.1 Titles

Ajaw

This is the universal Maya term for the king or supreme ruler of a city-state polity, a personage imbued with divinity – hence the prefix that reads

k'uhul, "holy," in the Emblem Glyph (see **5.1**). Ajaw as a title takes several forms; these are *not* to be confused with the day-sign Ajaw, which is always contained in a cartouche.

Glyphic forms of Ajaw:

The so-called "ben-ich" superfix, usually expressing the final Ajaw in an Emblem Glyph; but is also found in other expressions. It is generally read last in the expressions.

The "full" form of the "ben-ich" superfix, here drawn with optional phonetic complements **a-** and **-w(a)**. Maya scribes apparently considered this glyph to be present in every compound which carried the "ben-ich" superfix, with the large "main sign" hidden behind, for instance, the *Mutal* "bundle" in the Tik'al Emblem Glyph.

The Vulture form, often with a cartouche-less Ajaw day-sign or "Jester God" (a foliate-head diadem so-called because of its resemblance to a European Medieval jester with his protuberated hat) on the forehead. The Vulture main sign may also be preceded by the *k'uhul* glyph, and supervised by the "ben-ich" form of *ajaw*.

The "Young Lord" form. This is the head of the youthful Hero Twin Hunahpu (**11.3**), with its telltale spotted cheek. Again, the Ajaw day-sign is fixed to the forehead.

With the female agentive prefix **IX-** added this is also the title for queens or principal wives of the ruler:

   IX ["k'atun"] AJAW *Ix ("k'atun") Ajaw* "Queen 'K'atun'"

K'inich

Once misread *mak'inah* on the basis of its apparently transparent syllabograms, this entire collocation is now known to be a single logogram **K'INICH** *K'inich*, translated as "Great Sun." The title, which was common only at Palenque and Caracol, appears immediately before or after the name of the Ajaw or king, and behaves like part of the royal name.

1   2   3

K'INICH K'UK'-BAHLAM-m(a) *K'inich K'uk'-Bahlam* "Great Sun Quetzal-Jaguar" (name of Palenque king)

Kaloomte'

The title of *Kaloomte'* – once wrongly read as *Batab* (actually a Colonial Yukatek title) – may follow the names of only the most powerful Ajaws, those

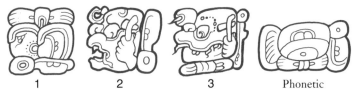

1   2   3   Phonetic

who ruled the largest and most influential kingdoms. Perhaps it bore a meaning similar to our "autocrat." The title is sometimes preceded by the glyph for the direction "west" (**12.1.1**), seemingly an allusion to Teotihuacan in central Mexico, the great city that supplied the militaristic ideology of the Maya kings.

1   2   West *Kaloomte'*

Ch'ok

If a personal name is followed by this title

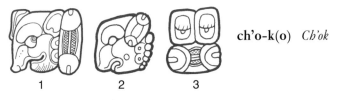

1   2   3   **ch'o-k(o)** *Ch'ok*

it signifies that that individual is a prince and perhaps an heir apparent – or, in the case of women, a princess. This is a remarkably regular expression, always being written with the same syllabograms, and is easy to recognize. The *Ch'ok* title is based on the word *ch'ok*, which means something like "unripe" or "immature" in the Ch'olan languages.

Sajal

Subsidiary war leaders or perhaps provincial governors were called by the title *Sajal*.

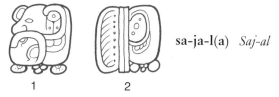

sa-ja-l(a) *Saj-al*

1   2

Relief scenes show them taking captives along with their superiors, the kings. They seem to have governed subsidiary centers away from the capital. Since they were subordinates, they could be "possessed" by the king, using the pronoun ⬡ *u-*.

The wife of a Sajal was termed *Ix Sajal*, the usual glyph taking the ⬡ IX- agentive prefix. It should be added that on the testimony of lintels at Yaxchilan, at least some royal women actually *were* Sajals.

The "captives" title

Boasting about the number of captives they had taken during their military careers, or about especially famous prisoners, is often featured in the string of titles that may appear after the ruler's name. The usual formula is **AJ-(number)-BAAK**, "he of the X captives," as in this often-repeated title of the Yaxchilan ruler "Bird Jaguar":

AJ-(20)-BAAK *aj (20)-baak* "he of the 20 captives"

Here the "moon-sign" is the glyph for "20"; and the "bone" sign is the logogram for "prisoner."

"Ajaw k'atuns"

For rulers who were middle-aged or older – a definite feat considering the ubiquity of warfare – the scribe would sometimes add the Ajaw title (one of the logograms for *Ajaw*, "king") on top of a k'atun glyph. The bar-and-dot coefficient before it tells which k'atun of his life the ruler was currently in. Here is an "Ajaw k'atun" expression for a ruler who was between about 40 and 60 years old:

OX-(k'atun)-AJAW "the 3-k'atuns king"

An analogous numbered k'atun could appear with other royal titles, in this case for a ruler over 80 years old:

HO-(k'atun)-ch'a-jo-m(a)
"the 5-k'atuns *ch'ajom*" (an undeciphered title)

u-baah and Bakab

Strings of names and titles are very often "framed" by *u-baah* and *Bakab* glyph compounds. In fact, *u-baah* is a kind of introductory glyph announcing that an important personal name is to follow. It consists of the **u-** 3rd-person-singular possessive pronoun (his/her), a gopher's head (**ba**) below the syllabogram **hi**, and means something like "his/her person" or "himself/her-self"). You will find it throughout the inscriptions and on pictorial vases.

1 **u-BAAH-hi** *u-baah*
2 **u-BAAH** *u-baah*

Placed at the very close of entire nominal phrases (names, titles, and Emblem Glyphs) in the inscriptions on both monuments and pottery is the ubiquitous but little-understood title written **ba-ka-b(a)**, *bakab*. According to Bishop Landa and other early Colonial sources, the Maya of Yukatan believed that the Bakabs were four divine brothers whose task was to hold up the sky. Perhaps the Bakab title magnified royalty by placing them in the role of sky-bearers.

ba-ka-b(a)

Royal women added the **IX-** prefix to the *bakab* title.

Aj Pitz

Maya kings were often shown playing ball in stone-built courts or against stairs, and they were proud of their athletic prowess. Accordingly, in the royal inscriptions some took on the title *aj pitz*,

"He of the Ballgame" or "the Ballplayer."

6.2 Rulers

The list of all the rulers of every major Maya city-state cannot be given here, but we will list the most important ones – those that you are most likely to encounter on your travels, in museum exhibits, and in books (*ill.* 7). Remember that in many instances we don't know how these nominal glyphs actually sounded to the ancient Maya – only where we have syllabic substitutions or obvious phonetic complements to the logograms can we be sure. Nicknames for glyphic names are those given by modern Mayanists (some of them not even epigraphers), and probably bear no relation to the true reading, which has yet to be discovered. They will be left in quotes. The dates given represent accession to the throne and death, where these are known; they are all AD. Readers who wish to follow up this subject in depth should consult Martin and Grube 2000.

As with the titles, almost all women's names in both monumental and ceramic texts are prefixed by the female agentive pronoun **IX-**.

Major kings of the Classic Maya

Tik'al

Chak Tok Ich'aak I

Yax Nuun Ayiin I

Siyaj Chan K'awiil II

K'an Chitam

Jasaw Chan K'awiil I ("Ruler A")

Yik'in (?) Chan K'awiil

Chak Tok Ich'aak I	360 – 378
Yax Nuun Ayiin I	379 – 404?
Siyaj Chan K'awiil II	411 – 456
K'an Chitam	458 – 486?
Jasaw Chan K'awiil I	682 – 734
Yik'in (?) Chan K'awiil	734 – 746

Naranjo

K'ak' Tiliw Chan Chaak

K'ak' Tiliw Chan Chaak	693 – *c.* 728

Palenque

1

2

K'inich Janaab Pakal ("the Great")

3

Janaab Pakal

K'inich Kan Bahlam II

K'inich K'an Joy Chitam II

1   2

Ahkal Mo' Naab

3   4   5

K'inich Ahkal Mo' Naab III

K'inich K'uk' Bahlam II

K'inich Janaab' Pakal ("the Great")	615 – 683
K'inich Kan Bahlam II	684 – 702
K'inich K'an Joy Chitam II	702 – 711
K'inich Ahkal Mo' Naab III	721 – c. 736
K'inich K'uk' Bahlam II	764 – c. 783

Yaxchilan

1   2

Itzamnaaj Bahlam II

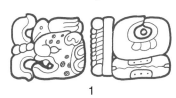
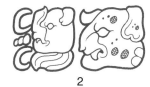

1   2

Yaxuun-Bahlam IV   ya-xu-ni BAHLAM

Itzamnaaj Bahlam II ("Shield Jaguar")	681 – 742
Yaxuun Bahlam IV/"Bird Jaguar"	752 – 768

Note. Yaxuun is the Maya name for a blue bird, the Lovely Cotinga.

Bonampak

Yajaw Chan Muwaan

Yajaw Chan Muwaan   ? – ?

Copan

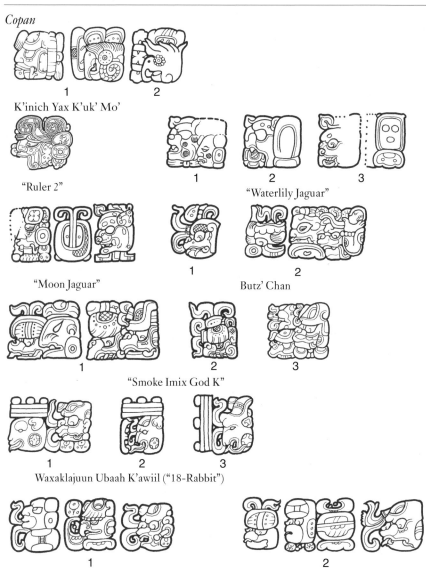

1   2

K'inich Yax K'uk' Mo'

"Ruler 2"

1   2   3

"Waterlily Jaguar"

1

"Moon Jaguar"

1   2

Butz' Chan

1   2   3

"Smoke Imix God K"

1   2   3

Waxaklajuun Ubaah K'awiil ("18-Rabbit")

1   2

K'ak' Joplaj Chan K'awiil   ("Smoke Monkey")

K'ak' Yipyaj Chan K'awiil ("Smoke Shell")

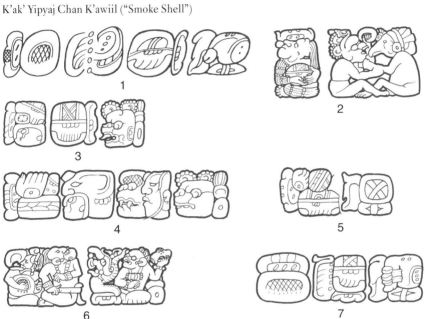

Yax Pasaj Chan Yoaat

K'inich Yax K'uk' Mo'	426 – *c.* 437
"Ruler 2"	*c.* 437 – ?
"Waterlily Jaguar"	*c.* 504 – *c.* 544
"Moon Jaguar"	553 – 578
Butz' Chan	578 – 628
"Smoke Imix God K"	628 – 695
Waxaklajuun Ubaah K'awiil	695 – 738
K'ak' Joplaj Chan K'awiil	738 – 749
K'ak' Yipyaj Chan K'awiil	749 – *c.* 761
Yax Pasaj Chan Yoaat	763 – *c.* 820

Quiriguá

| 1 | 2 |

K'ak' Tiliw Chan Yoaat

K'ak' Tiliw Chan Yoaat   724 – 785

EXERCISE 7

You now have enough information to read nominal expressions in the inscriptions of some well-known and often-visited Maya cities. Here are two:

Who was this man, where did he rule, what had he done, and what was his approximate age? Note: as with most actual Maya inscriptions, some details have been lost, but you should be able to read the glyphs anyway.

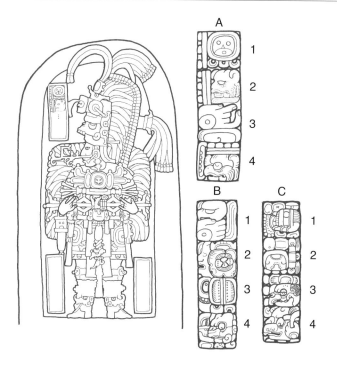

The subject matter of this well-known stela is a richly-garbed standing lord, holding a "ceremonial bar" in his arms. Who is he, where is he from, and what title does he bear? Can you work out the date, and what was its significance?

Answers on page 170

7

RELATIONSHIPS

Since provable or fictive descent from distinguished ancestors – even from gods – was necessary to demonstrate one's right to assume the powers of royalty and nobility during Classic times, it is little wonder that parentage and other kinship relations figure importantly in the inscriptions. Even in late pre-Conquest Yukatan, to be noble, *al-mehen*, was to be able to trace one's ancestry in both the female (*al*) and male (*mehen*) lines.

So much for lineage and descent. But almost as important were affiliations based on marriage, since through this institution one city-state could establish binding ties with even far-flung domains. In a sociopolitical landscape in which wars were constantly being fought, marriage alliances as well as diplomacy were crucial to survival of the body politic – and to the personal survival of potential combatants.

7.1 Parentage statements

As did the late Yukatek Maya, the Classic Maya scribes distinguished between descent from a mother and descent from a father. Where both parents are named, the mother is first, then the father, as in the Yukatek *al-mehen*. Here are the relevant glyphs for parentage statements:

"Child of woman"

The "child of woman" glyph has several variants, but it is always prefixed by ya- as a 3rd-person-singular possessive for a noun that begins with the vowel *a-*. The main sign of the glyph is sometimes an open hand holding either a **la** sign (an "inverted Ajaw") or another small glyph.

Alternatively, the main sign might be the **la** syllabogram by itself. In any event, it corresponds to *y-al*, "child of (female)":

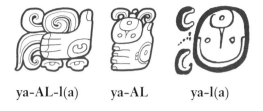

ya-AL-l(a) ya-AL ya-l(a)

"Child of man"

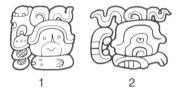

1   2

Here the main sign resembles the Ajaw day-sign; it is often surmounted by the so-called "smoke" affix; below may be any one of several suffixes, most often **-IL**. The reading is still unknown, but since it almost always appears prefixed with the possessive **u-**, it must mean "the child of (male personage)." There is a substitute that *can* actually be read:

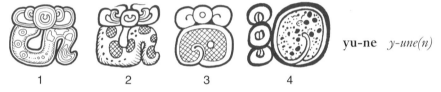

1   2   3   4

yu-ne *y-une(n)*

This form spells *y-unen*, "the child/baby of."

7.2 Spouse

Inexplicably, the marriages of rulers receive little notice in the Classic inscriptions, even though women obviously played a highly significant role in elite society, and often appear in rituals depicted on the monuments. Nevertheless we do have a glyph for "spouse," first recognized by Floyd Lounsbury in the Dresden Codex. This consists of a "crossed bands" main sign, subfixed by the **na** syllabogram as a phonetic complement, and prefixed by **ya-** , the required possessive pronoun. The combination is read *y-atan*, "his/her spouse":

ya-AT-AN *y-atan* "the spouse of…"

7.3 Siblings

All of the Mayan languages have separate words for "elder brother" and "younger brother," and so did Classic Mayan. The respective terms are *sukun* (or *sakun*) *winik* and *itz'in winik*. The second member of each phrase, *winik*, is the generic word for "person," with the phonetic complements **wi** and **k(i)**.

 su-ku(n)-WINIK-k(i) *sukun winik* "elder brother"

 sa-ku(n)-wi-WINIK-k(i) *sakun winik* "elder brother"

 i-tz'i(n)-WINIK *itz'in winik* "younger brother"

 **yi-tz'i(n) wi-WINIK-k(i)** *yitz'in winik* "his younger brother"

8

WARFARE

Archaeologists used to think that the Classic Maya were a peaceful people, ruled by benevolent theocrats – this, in the face of abundant evidence on the monuments depicting warriors with shields and spears, and captives being trampled underfoot and otherwise debased by their proud conquerors. But the decipherment of the Classic texts has changed all this. Warfare was carried on throughout the Maya realm, one city-state pitted against another, less for the idea of territorial gain than for the prestige of gaining noble prisoners to be sacrificed to the gods. The vocabulary of war and the struggle for hegemony is to be found everywhere in the hieroglyphic texts. In fact, the "capture" glyph (*chukaj,* "he is captured") was one of the first to be deciphered by Yuri Knorosov in the early 1950s. The beginning student might well concentrate on stelae and other reliefs that celebrate victories and the capture of enemies, for these texts are the easiest to grasp for neophytes in hieroglyphic studies. Just look for the shield and spear, and the unfortunate prisoner who usually grovels below his new master.

8.1 Glyphs for general war

One verbal compound over all others expresses the total event of warfare waged against another city-state. This is the "star-war" event, consisting of the "star" sign with falling droplet extensions, placed over the syllabic sign **yi**:

It cannot yet be read, but it *is* a verb since it can take the verbal suffix **-YA**. The "star-war" glyph is usually placed before or even over the main sign of the enemy city's Emblem Glyph, as in these examples:

[war against Naranjo]   [war against Seibal]

 [war against Yaxha]

Another compound also expresses the idea of war, but in couplet form (a common literary device in Mesoamerica): the "flint-shield" glyph or glyph compound, consisting of the logogram or syllabic signs for *took'*, "flint," and the logogram or syllabograms for *pakal*, "shield" (*ill. 10*). This expresses the use of flint-tipped spears and darts, and hand-held shields, in warrior-to-warrior combat.

 TOOK'-PAKAL *took'- pakal* "flint-shield"

 u-to-k'(a) u-pa-ka-l(a) *u-took' u-pakal* "his flint, his shield"

8.2 The taking of prisoners

The capture, display, and eventual sacrifice of prominent enemies was an obsession of the typical Ajaw, events that were commemorated on untold numbers of Classic Maya monuments, in both pictorial and glyphic form. Following the date, the overwhelming majority of "capture" expressions begin with the verb root ***chuhk***, "to capture, seize," most often in the present passive form:

 chu(h)-k(a)-AJ *chuhk-aj* "he is captured"

Then follows the name of the unfortunate captive, a personage of noble if not royal rank, to which may be added one of the "captive" glyphs given below. The sentence ends with the name and titles of the captor – who is either an *ajaw* or a *sajal*.

Basking in the glory of his conquests, the militarily successful king was fond of having his scribes celebrate his prowess by constant references to his prisoner or prisoners. There were three ways to do this glyphically:

1   by placing the name of the captive before the expression *u-baak*:

u-ba-k(i)   *u-baak*
his prisoner" or "he is his prisoner"

2   by the *u-cha'an* expression, just before the name of the prisoner:

u-CHA'AN(?)-nu   *u-cha'an*   "master of...(?)..."

3   by inserting the "count of captives" expression in the string of titles following the name of a great king or *sajal*. This takes the form of the male agentive *aj*, then the number, and finally a sign for *baak*, as in the following examples:

1 **AJ-2-BAAK**   *aj-cha-baak*   "he of the two captives"
2 **AJ-5-BAAK**   *aj-ho-baak*   "he of the five captives"
3 **AJ-5-ba-k(i)**   *aj-ho-baak*   "he of the five captives"

4 **AJ-20-BAAK**   *aj-k'al-baak*
"he of the 20 captives" (a favorite title of the renowned "Bird-Jaguar" IV of Yaxchilan)

EXERCISE 8

Now you have enough information to understand and perhaps even translate a major Maya monument, in this case the famous Lintel 8 from Yaxchilan. Transcribe and transliterate the text as best you can, and give a complete translation. *Hints*: the standard lettering of columns does not reflect the sense of the text. What is the historical event pictured here, and who are the actors?

EXERCISE 9

These four texts are carved on the supports for Altar 2 at the great city of Piedras Negras, on the Guatemalan side of the Usumacinta River. All 36 glyphs form a continuous text that opens at A1–B1. This is a Calendar Round date 7 Men 18 K'ank'in corresponding to the Long Count position 9.13.9.14.15 (18 November 701 in the Julian Calendar). Work out the remaining Calendar Rounds, along with their respective Long Count positions, and describe the significance of each date, including the first.

Note: don't try to transcribe the glyphs at B2–A3, D3–F1, H3, and L2. They are all names of a single ruler, known to epigraphers only as "Ruler 4."

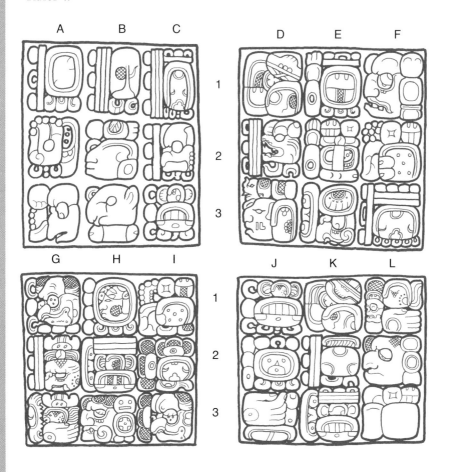

Answers on pages 170–171

9

SCRIBES AND ARTISTS

One of the unforeseen but happy developments arising from the past 15 years of Maya glyphic research has been a very detailed picture of the role played by scribes and artists in the cultural and social life of the Classic Maya – their titles, functions, gods, and even, in many cases, their personal names. We now know that these gifted people occupied an exalted social position in the Maya city-states, and that their duties probably covered more than the arts of carving, writing, and painting. In fact, the Classic Maya scribe may well have played the same role as the priest (*Aj K'in*) in late pre-Conquest Yukatan, described by Landa and other early sources.

9.1 Users of brush pens

As shall be seen here, the signatures of great Maya artists appear on Late Classic stone monuments of a number of centers, particularly in the Usumacinta River drainage, but artist-scribes were also proud to put their names and titles on Late Classic pictorial vases. We shall show you how to recognize these on stelae as well as on carved or painted vases. You should first of all understand certain distinctions. Most importantly, in Classic Mayan and throughout the Mayan linguistic family, exactly the same word is used for "writing" and for "painting." This is *tz'ib*, written thus:

 tz'i-b(i) *tz'ib* "writing, painting"

Adding the male proclitic *aj-* to this glyph produced the title of a painter or scribe:

Standard   Adjectival Form   Logographic variant

1 **AJ-tz'i-b(i)** *aj-tz'ib*
2 **AJ-tz'i-b(a) (-li)** *aj-tz'ib(-al)*
3 **AJ-TZ'IB-b(a)** *aj-tz'ib*
"the scribe, the painter"

The noun *tz'ib* may also take the 3rd-person-possessive pronoun, in which case the name of the scribe sometimes follows:

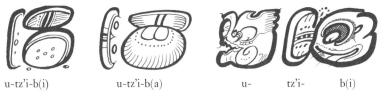

| u-tz'i-b(i) | u-tz'i-b(a) | u- | tz'i- | b(i) |

u-tz'ib "his writing" (or "his painting")

This phrase often appears in the **Primary Standard Sequence (PSS)** written on fine, painted ceramics (see **10.2**).

9.2 Carvers

In contrast to those who used brushes or brush pens along with ink or pigments to work their art were the carvers of glyphs and scenes on stone monuments, such as stelae and lintels, along with those artists who carved or incised ceramic vases. The glyphic compound which always introduces their names is not yet well understood, but it is regularly prefixed by syllabic **yu**, and consists of a bat head which probably reads **xu** plus the syllabogram **lu**; sometimes the **lu** precedes the bat head, and occasionally follows it; on the monuments, however, it is usually conflated within it (*ill. 5*). Therefore, except for the **yu** (which probably represents the 3rd person possessive followed by an *u-* vowel), the reading order is not known for sure. Epigraphers refer to it either as the "*lu*-Bat expression," or read it as *yuxul*, "his carving."

Here are two variations on the "*lu*-Bat" theme, the first from a monument, the second from a carved vase:

| 1 | 2 |

Look for such signatures away from the main text, often but not always in an inconspicuous position in recessed areas, and customarily on a smaller scale than the principal text.

Example:

Some monuments are signed by more than one sculptor, each of these having distinctive "handwriting." A good example of this phenomenon is Stela 34 from El Perú, a massive carving now in the Cleveland Museum of Art. Here are the eight signatures, scattered over the stela's surface (note that two of these artists took the *ajaw* royal title):

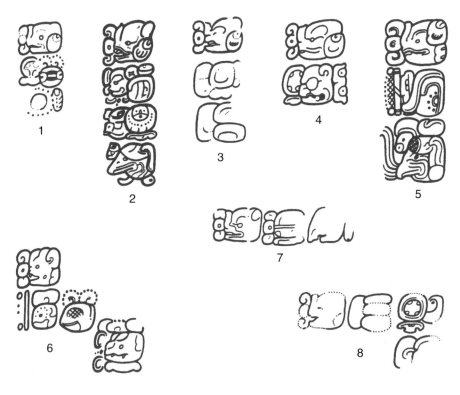

Drawing by David Stuart

9.3 Other titles for artists and scribes

The aforesaid glyph compounds introduce the names of scribes and artists, and distinguish between the two main categories of them, but there are other honorific titles that were bestowed on these prestigious individuals, some of them perhaps reflecting wider responsibilities within the city-state polity. The easiest one to understand is *itz'aat*, "artist, sage":

i-tz'a-t(a) *itz'at* "artist"
Note: the first part of the glyph is a conflation of **i** and **tz'a**.

A far more complex matter is this still-controversial glyphic title, which has several variations:

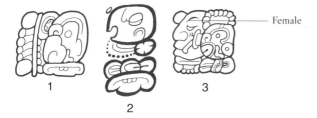

Nikolai Grube reads this as **AJ-K'UH-HUN-n(a)**, *aj-k'uh-huun*, and translates it as something like "he of the holy paper" (i.e., codices or royal headbands). The officials to whom this title was applied always wear a highly distinctive costume, including a sarong, unkempt hair bound in a cloth, and an object bound to the forehead that looks very much like a bunch of quill pens. Although these personages were of very high status, they could also be "possessed" by the sovereign, their employer. In many cases, on both pottery and on the monuments, they seem be acting as masters of ceremonies.

10

CERAMIC TEXTS

10.1 General remarks

Unless you can actually travel to the ancient Maya ruins, you are most likely to encounter Maya hieroglyphic writing in public museums, painted or carved on fine Classic period ceramics. It used to be claimed that such texts were meaningless, since it was alleged that they had been turned out by illiterate, peasant artists who had exploited the glyphs only for their decorative value. This turns out to be completely wrong: not only are most of the pottery texts highly meaningful, but the painters and carvers involved were completely literate, and of very high status.

We have to distinguish between two kinds of texts. **Primary** texts appear in bands encircling the exterior just below the rim, or in some other prominent place, while **Secondary** ones appear within the scene depicted, sometimes in L-shaped boxes like those on the monuments. The important thing to remember is this: *the primary texts almost never have any direct connection with the activities or principal actors in the scenes below, while the secondary texts describe or modify such scenes and/or actors.* It is in the secondary texts that one can find the use of everyday conversation, very frequently indicated by a device which recalls the "balloons" of recorded speech in comic strips – here, on pottery vessels, you will see wispy "speech scrolls" connecting the human or supernatural actors to the texts. The secondary texts probably reflect what must have been the highly sophisticated narratives of the now-disappeared Classic codices.

It is thus no surprise to occasionally encounter first- and second-person statements in the secondary texts; the investigation of these represents a frontier in epigraphic research.

The secondary texts frequently "name names," and it from these that most of our knowledge concerning the *way*, the monstrous alter-ego spirits of the royal family, are derived (see **11.7**).

10.2 The Primary Standard Sequence (PSS)

The most common of all Maya hieroglyphic texts is *not* the Initial Series carved on monuments, as one might expect, but the **Primary Standard Sequence** or **PSS**, a highly formulaic text that always occupies a primary position on ceramics and, very infrequently, on monuments. If you see a beautiful painted or carved vase or bowl in a museum, always look for this text, which is usually present. Since it is customarily wrapped around the rim of the vessel, the trick is to find out where it begins. If the **PSS** is lengthy, the solution is to locate the **Initial Sign,**  of which there are many

variants and which generally opens the text, but if it is truncated, sometimes the first glyph is the "Wing-Quincunx" sign (see below).

1   2

The complete **PSS** sequence contains about a dozen glyphs, but there are very few examples in which all appear together; however, no matter how few or how many, they always appear in the same order. Some of the glyphs have been satisfactorily deciphered, others less so. The difficulties of reading them perhaps stem from the fact that this formula is so very ancient – how many Americans, for instance, understand the meaning of *e pluribus unum* on their pennies, let alone *novus ordo seclorum* on the dollar bill?

There are three parts to the **PSS**, always in the same order:

1 *The vessel dedication.* This opens with the Initial Sign, *alay*, "this,"

1   2   3   4   5   6

a pronoun with -ya suffix, which is followed by one of two alternative glyphs. The first of these is the head of "Pawahtuun," also called God N,

1   2   3

an old god of the four directions of the world, often with a  -**yi** suffix, while the second is the so-called "Step" glyph. Both appear to read *t'abay*, "to ascend."

Conflated
with God N

1   2   3

Occasionally, another glyph may appear here, either alone or preceding the "Pawahtuun." This bears the nickname "Flat Hand" and may describe the presentation part of a ceremony of the vessel's consecration (the same verb appears in descriptions of "stone-tying" ceremonies at Period Endings (see **4.3.1**)).

1   2

The gist of these glyphs is apparently, "It was raised..."
Then may appear the *tz'ib* or writing glyph,

usually prefixed with or u-, giving the reading *u-tz'ib*, "his writing"; usually rendered as a verbal phrase, "He writes it," possibly indicated by the verbal ending -**naj** and/or containing the noun-derivative ending -**IL**. This glyph may either take the standard form (see **9.1**), or it may be "written out" with a bat-head **tz'i**, followed by a **b(i)** or **b(a)**:

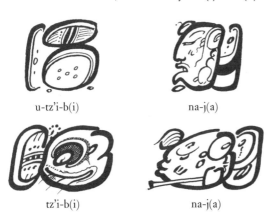

u–tz'i–b(i)   na–j(a)

tz'i–b(i)   na–j(a)

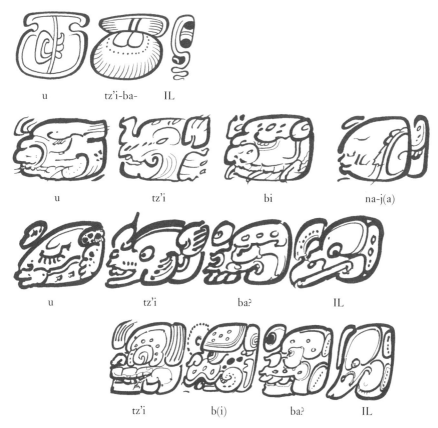

u	tz'i-ba-	IL	

u	tz'i	bi	na-j(a)

u	tz'i	ba?	IL

tz'i	b(i)	ba?	IL

The next glyph modifies the verb *u-tz'ib*. It may follow *u-tz'ib*, and read *hich* "surface," but more commonly *yich* "its surface" precedes the verb. This difficult phrase reads something like "...was painted, the surface" or "...the surface for writing"

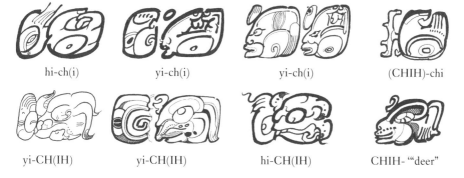

hi-ch(i)	yi-ch(i)	yi-ch(i)	(CHIH)-chi

yi-CH(IH)	yi-CH(IH)	hi-CH(IH)	CHIH- "deer"

It is at this point that the name of the scribe or painter, and even his parentage, may appear. However, if this is a carved pot, then the "*lu*-Bat" glyph ("his carving?") will be substituted (see **9.2**).

1   2

2 *The shape of the vessel.* Here there are three possibilities. If this is a relatively tall, cylindrical vase or a deep bowl, the "Wing- Quincunx" glyph appears:

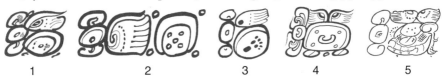

1   2   3   4   5

this is read as **yu-k'i-b(i)**, *yu-k'ib*, "his/her vessel for drink." You will almost certainly encounter this glyph on such vessels, which were generally used to hold the chocolate drink; sometimes it leads off the **PSS** statement. If the vessel is a plate, then the glyph in this position is

u-la-k(a) *u-lak* "his/her plate."

1   2   3

If such a plate has three legs, then it may be termed a

ja-wa(n)-TE' *jawante'* "tripod dish."

Both of these flat-bottomed ceramic forms were used to hold tamales.

3 *The contents of the vessel.* In all but a very few examples, the *yu-k'ib* glyph is followed by the sign for chocolate:

1   2   3

This is generally spelled **ka-ka-w(a)**, *kakaw*, "chocolate," and may be prefixed by one or more signs describing what kind or flavor of chocolate is in the vase (*ill. 15*):

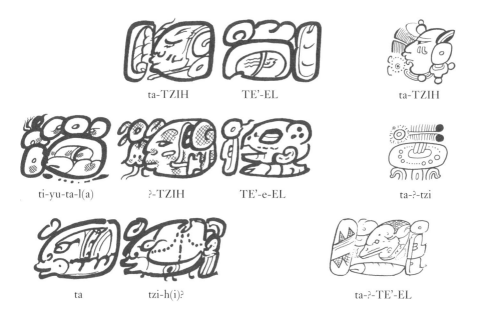

ta-TZIH	TE'-EL		ta-TZIH
ti-yu-ta-l(a)	?-TZIH	TE'-e-EL	ta-?-tzi
ta	tzi-h(i)?		ta-?-TE'-EL

For example, **ta-TZIH-TE'-EL,** *ta tzih te'el,* may mean "fresh from the tree."

A few deep, rounded bowls substitute the glyph for the sacred, gruel-like drink *atole*, written **u-l(u)**, *ul,* "*atole.*"

We present on the following four pages a number of examples of the **PSS** from Late Classic vessels, both painted and carved; these will give the reader some idea of the great artistic latitude allowed the scribe in writing this text. Please bear in mind that the painter/carver/scribe may have written only key glyphs within the **PSS** sequence; how many were expressed probably was the choice of the patron, but no single vessel gives them all.

After the **PSS** come the names and titles of the patron or owner of the vessel; if the personage was a royal, then the entire text – the **PSS** plus the owner's nominal phrase – might end in an Emblem Glyph and

 a *bakab* expression (see **6.1**) (*ill. 14*).

Thus, in a way the **PSS** is an extensive case of what epigraphers call **name-tagging**, giving an object's name along with that of its possessor; such name-tagged objects may include whole buildings, parts of buildings, and even monuments, so it is no surprise that elements of the **PSS** may be found carved on them, too.

Various examples of the PSS

a-LAY-y(a)   "Pawahtuun"   tz'i-b(i)   na-j(a)   hi-ch(i)

a-LAY-y(a)   "Step"   u-tz'i-b(i)-   na-j(a)

a-LAY-y(a)   "Step +Pawahtuun"   u   tz'i   b(i)

a-LAY-y(a)   "Flat-hand"   yi-CH(IH)   yu-lu-??-IL

a-LAY-y(a)   "Pawahtuun"   yi-ch(i)   u   tz'i-ba-   l(i)

a-LAY-y(a)   "Step"

yu-k'i-b(i)   ti-yu-ta-l(a)   ka-ka-wa

u   ja-wa-TE'   ti-u-l(u)

na-j(a)   yu-k'i-b(i)   ta   -tzi   ??-TE'-EL

yu-k'i-b(i)   ta-??-le-TE'   ka(kaw)

yu-k'i-b(i)-l(a)   ta-TZIH   sa-AL-l(a)   ka-ka-

Various examples of the PSS continued

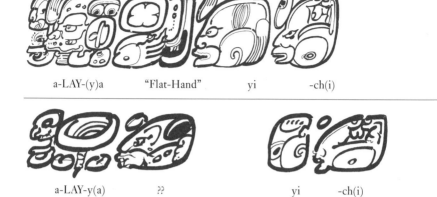

| a-LAY-(y)a | "Flat-Hand" | yi | -ch(i) |

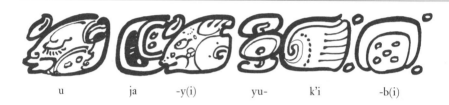

| a-LAY-y(a) | ?? | | yi | -ch(i) |

| u | ja | -y(i) | yu- | k'i | -b(i) |

Note: Every surviving **PSS** contains only a portion of the "complete" sequence of 20-odd glyphs. Few examples are longer than eight or ten glyphs; many abbreviate it to three or four. The reason for this condensation is unknown; it could be simply another example of *pars pro toto*. For this reason we have composed the eight examples given above from several sources. We have deleted the names and titles that often conclude a **PSS** and concentrated on the parts of the texts that are common to most of these vessels.

Our first three samples on pages 104–105 are from Late Classic "Codex-style" vessels. The fourth example comes from a spectacular Middle Classic red-and-black engraved *uk'ib* (drinking vessel) – the use of the "carving" rather than "writing" collocation in the fourth glyph reflects the carved rather than painted text.

We distilled the fifth and sixth lines from several Early Classic vessels of Tikal and elsewhere, since early texts tend to be quite abbreviated.

The final three examples both come from a single Waxaktun-style vase. Waxaktun artists sometimes, unaccountably, painted two **PSS**'s on the same vessel. The first (our seventh line) is in very large and ornate glyphs, the second (eighth and ninth lines) much smaller and simpler, but one of the longest known **PSS**'s. They are not drawn to scale.

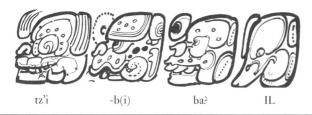

| tz'i | -b(i) | ba? | IL |

| u | tz'i | ba? | IL |

| ta | tzi | -y(i)? |

EXERCISE 10

This is a **PSS** rim text from a Late Classic polychrome vase (K1941 in the Kerr Archive). What was the purpose of the vase? Can you identify the name, gender, and city-state of the person named in the text?

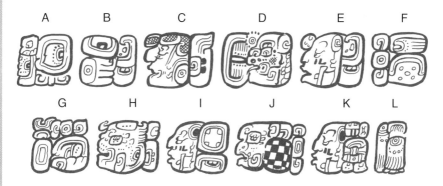

A   B   C   D   E   F

G   H   I   J   K   L

Answers on page 171

11

THE SUPERNATURAL WORLD

11.1 General remarks

Although, as in many cultures other than our own, there is no Maya word for "religion," the Maya were and still are a deeply religious people. To the pre-Conquest Maya, the supernatural world was as real and tangible as the everyday world that our senses can perceive, and all of their behavior was oriented towards it. There was a pantheon of major gods, some of them intimately connected with the agricultural round and with daily life, and some with the concerns of the elite and the royal lineage. Such divinities have their counterparts elsewhere in Mesoamerica, such as among the Aztecs of central Mexico (where the Aztec god of rain and lightning, Tlaloc, is the clear relative of the Maya Chaak), but others were far more localized to specific Maya cities and the territory they controlled.

The supernatural world also included a host of lesser supernaturals that one might even term "demons," particularly the *way* (see **11.7**) that functioned as spirit alter-egos to members of the ruling caste.

All of these sacred beings appear in glyphic form on the monuments and in the surviving codices; in fact, the four books are exclusively concerned with the world of the gods, and rituals performed in their honor. As far back as 1897 the German scholar Paul Schellhas made a highly successful attempt to organize the various representations in the manuscripts into an array of deities, to each of which he gave a letter designation (A for the principal Death God, B for the Rain God Chaak, and so on), and to identify the name glyph or glyphs for each. We still use his system, with modification in the light of more recent evidence, especially in the case of gods for whom we have not yet discovered a convincing name in the books or in the inscriptions (God L is an excellent example, see **11.3**).

Although a few deity names could be written syllabically, the usual practice was to indicate the god by means of a logogram based upon the head of that particular being, with the iconographic markings and other attributes that distinguish it from others in the same supernatural class. Some of these logograms are as old as the beginning of the Early Classic and even older, and more than a few remain phonetically opaque.

Bishop Landa tells us that in late pre-Conquest times in Yukatan, certain gods were quadripartite, that is, the godhead simultaneously existed at the four cardinal directions, in *four* distinct forms, each associated with a certain color. We know that such fourfold gods included Chaak, "Pawahtuun," and probably K'awiil in his role as Bakab (all this will be described in **11.3**). Associations of otherwise distinct gods, usually in groups of *three*, or **Triads** (**11.5**), seem to have been tutelary deities of cities like Palenque, Tik'al, and Caracol, and – at least at Palenque – played an important part in the local creation myth. And finally, some very important gods were *paired*, expressing primary cosmic oppositions such as sky vs. earth, light vs. darkness, and the like.

There are certain features that immediately distinguish gods from mortals:

- Older deities, such as the supreme god Itzamnaaj, usually have large, goggle-like "god-eyes," and sometimes prominent front teeth.

- Young deities, and occasionally even the older ones, have "god-markings" along the outer borders of their limbs and torsos, to make it clear that they are not to be considered human. These markings are actually glyphic elements, most often symbolizing bright, shiny mirrors, or dark (obsidian) ones.

11.2 Divinity and godhead

The general word for "divinity" or "god" in Classic Mayan is *k'uh*, while the adjectival form is *k'uhul*, with the meaning "sacred" or "holy." The logogram for both noun and adjective takes the form of a monkey-like profile head prefixed by the so-called "Water Group" affix:

K'UH *k'uh* "god"; or
K'UHUL *k'uhul* "holy"

K'uhul may introduce the name of an individual god in a text, and ceramic texts are known in which it appears before the names of each god in a long series of named divinities.

In the fully written-out Emblem Glyph, the "Water Group" prefix alone appears to the left of the polity's main sign plus the affixes spelling *ajaw*, "king":

K'UHUL BAAK-AL AJAW   *k'uhul baakal ajaw*
"Holy King of Palenque"

A related term which may appear with the name glyphs of divine beings, including apotheosized rulers, can be translated as "his/her holy name," and takes the form of the **K'UH** head – minus the usual dotted prefix – within the bend of an elbow-shaped element known to be the logogram **K'ABA'**, "name." Sacred locations, such as temples, could also receive "holy names."

K'UHUL K'ABA   *k'uhul k'aba*   "holy name"

11.3   The major gods

In this brief manual, it would be impossible as well as impractical to give the name glyphs for all of the Maya gods that have been identified thus far. Accordingly, the reader will find here only those that are most frequently to be found in the Classic inscriptions, and to a lesser extent, in the codices. Those who wish a more exhaustive listing and description of the Maya supernatural world should refer to Taube's *The Major Gods of Ancient Yucatan* (1992), and to *The Gods and Symbols of Ancient Mexico and the Maya* by Mary Miller and Karl Taube (1993).

Chaak.   Originally designated "God B" by Schellhas, this ubiquitous god has long been known to be Chaak, the embodiment of lightning and thunder, and, by extension, the god of rain. In Classic iconography, he is recognized by the *Spondylus* shell worn over each ear, by his stubby, protruding upper lip, and by a tendril curling from each corner of the mouth. In full figure form, he carries a serpentine axe symbolizing his thunderbolt. Chaak is found throughout the Dresden and Madrid codices, where his upper lip is extended out to misleadingly resemble a long nose. Here are the Classic and Post-Classic (codical) forms of his name:

 CHAAK-k(i) *Chaak* "Chaak" (the Rain God)

 **cha-k(i)** (codex form of the above)

God GI. A highly significant divinity during most of the Classic period, this god is easy to confuse with Chaak. We have no idea of how his name was pronounced, or even of his function in Maya religion, but he seems to be associated with water – perhaps even the sea, since some of his traits are shark-like, and he may once, in Pre-Classic times, have been a shark god. In all events, he is the first ("GI") in the series of Palenque gods known as "the Triad" (**11.5**). Features by which he may be recognized are:

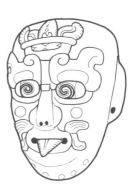

1   A large "god-eye" internally marked by a spiral line.
2   A *Spondylus* shell over each ear.
3   Fish fins or barbels on each side of the mouth.
4   A prominent, shark-like upper tooth.

Here is his name glyph:

1   2

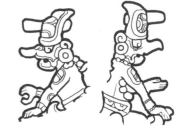

K'awiil. Known to Schellhas and to generations of scholars as "God K," this is the principal deity of the Maya royal line. The ubiquitous K'awiil is easily recognized by the following traits:

1   A large "god-eye."

2   The bright mirror device  in his forehead, from which juts either a tube emitting smoke, or an axe-blade.

3   One leg that terminates not in a foot but in a bearded serpent with open jaws, from which the head and shoulders of another deity might appear.

In displays of royal power, he is the "Mannikin Scepter" god grasped in rulers' hands during Period Ending ceremonies (see **4.3.1**). In the inscriptions, the K'awiil glyph – almost always a logogram – might be his full-figure form (as in the Palenque Triad (**11.5**)); his head; or the "smoking mirror" forehead device alone. The latter two may take a bar-and-dot "nine" (*bolon*) prefix, possibly indicating an alternate name for the god, *Bolon Tz'akab*, a name found in Landa's *Relación*.

| 1 | 2 | 3 | 4 | 5 |

K'inich Ajaw. This is the Sun God (Schellhas' "God G"), literally, the "Sun-eyed Ruler" or the "Sun-faced Ruler", recognizable by:

1   His large "god-eye," often distinctively marked with a pair of bent, somewhat squared, parallel lines in one corner of the eye.

2   A Roman nose.

3   Upper incisors filed into a T-shape.

4   A tendril curling from the corner of the mouth

5   Sometimes the flower-like **K'IN** logogram  in the forehead or
elsewhere. The **K'IN**-sign may also stand by itself as an indicator of
K'inich Ajaw.

In the monumental texts, K'inich Ajaw is most commonly found as the head
variant of the numerical coefficient "four."

1   2   3

Itzamnaaj. Once designated "God D," this deity is known
to be Itzamnaaj, the supreme creator deity, consort of
the old goddess Ix Chel (see below), and the originator
of writing. Itzamnaaj's iconographic traits are

1   A large "god-eye."

2   A Roman nose (typical of old gods).

3   Chop-fallen, somewhat toothless jaws,
indicating his aged status.

4   A device attached to the front of his
headdress, consisting of a circular, obsidian
mirror (the Akbal day-sign surrounded by
dots) and a pendant hanging from it; this
entire device, whether or not accompanied
by the deity's head, is read as the logogram **ITZAMNAAJ**.

The codical form of the name glyph takes the phonetic complement **na**.

1   2   3   4   5

ITZAMNAAJ-j(i) on monuments.

Form in Dresden Codex. **ITZAM-na**. *Itzamna* (probably the Post-Classic name for the deity).

God L. Unfortunately, we still don't know the name of this very important, aged divinity, who was a god both of merchants and of war among the Classic Maya, in spite of the fact that he often appears on pictorial pottery and in the codices. God L is frequently depicted smoking a cigar, so he may also be a patron of tobacco farmers. His distinguishing traits are

1   A broad-brimmed hat topped with black-tipped owl feathers and sometimes with the actual head of the bird in question.
2   A fringed cape ending in a point.
3   Sometimes a black face and body.
4   A large "god-eye" (not always present).
5   Chop-fallen jaws.

His name glyph, which cannot yet be read, is known only from the codices.

God L in the Dresden Codex.

God M. This is another merchant god, perhaps the Ek' Chuwah mentioned in Colonial sources. Found only in the Dresden and Madrid codices, both Late Post-Classic works, he is frequently conflated or otherwise confused with God L. Like God L, he is painted black, but has a Pinocchio-like or long, bulbous nose rather than a Roman one, and lacks the owl-feather sombrero of God L. God M's name glyph is seemingly absent in the Classic inscriptions:

God M in the Dresden Codex.

"Pawahtuun." Also known by the Schellhas designation as "God N," "Pawahtu-un" is an aged quadripartite divinity who  stands at the four corners of the universe, bearing on his raised hands both the earth and the sky. He also acts as the supernatural who presides over the end of the old year, and is a major patron of the scribes. In "Pawahtuun"'s best-known form, he exhibits most or all of the following traits:

1   A crenellated, netted headdress that may lean backwards or forwards.
2   The usual "god-eye" (but this is not always present).
3   A Roman nose.
4   A wrinkled face and toothless jaws.
5   Often a snail or turtle shell on the back, from which he sometimes may actually be emerging.

The head of "Pawahtuun," consisting of his profile along with the netted headdress, may occupy the second position in the Primary Standard Sequence (**10.2**), where it acts as a yet-undeciphered verb (see **1** below). With the **TUUN** sign substituting for the headdress, his profile visage becomes the Head Variant for the number "five" (see **2** below). In the codices (**3** and **4** below), his name glyph is written in logosyllabic form: in the superfix above the **TUUN** sign is the netted headdress flanking the "corn curl." To the left may be the number 4 or 5, for reasons unknown.

1   2   3   4

Note: The **TUUN** in this god's name is the year, not the "stone" sign.

The Maize God. This young and handsome god appears as "God E" in the Schellhas list. Thanks to iconographic discoveries by Taube, it is clear that he is cognate with Hun Hunahpu, the father of the Hero Twins in the Popol Vuh epic story. In Classic representations, apart from his obvious youth and his princely raiment, his salient features are the maize-coblike shape of his head; and on the top of his head, either maize foliage or a tonsure resembling corn silk. In the Classic monumental form, his head has maize foliage on top and the "corn curl" protruding from the forehead (this acts as the Head Variant for the number "eight"). In the codices, the relevant glyph is a very stylized Maize God head, somewhat foliated on top. Unfortunately, neither it nor its Classic forerunners can be *read*, even though we know their meaning.

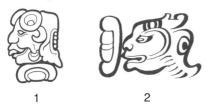

1   2

The Hero Twins. As the sons of the Maize God, these are intimately related with their father in both iconography and glyphs (*ill. 16*). Both are shown as good-looking young men, usually wearing white headbands; to make sure that no one would confuse them with ordinary humans, they have god-markings on their bodies and faces. In the case of Hun Ajaw (the Classic counterpart to Hunahpu of the Popol Vuh), these are black spots; his twin brother Yax Bahlam(?) (cognate with Xbalanque of the Popol Vuh) has patches of jaguar skin, especially over the lower part of the face, above a short beard. Their name glyphs reflect this iconography. The head of Hun Ajaw is a very common variant for the last day-sign, Ajaw, in the 260-day Count, and can be recognized by the black spot on the cheek. Yax Bahlam (?)'s glyph, with a **YAX** attachment, acts as the Head Variant of the number "nine."

HUN AJAW

1   2

 YAX BAHLAM(?)

Chak Chel. Now recognized as the same divinity as Ix Chel ("Lady Rainbow"), the goddess of weaving, childbirth, and medicine in Late Post-Classic Yukatan, the aged, somewhat sinister Chak Chel ("Great Rainbow") often appears on Classic pictorial vases, in the extant codices, and occasionally even on carved monuments. In the Schellhas classification, she is "Goddess O." Chak Chel may be the consort of the aged Itzamnaaj himself, and therefore a creator goddess. Her distinguishing features are:

1 Snakes and spindles in her hair.
2 An aged, toothless face.
3 Clawed hands and feet.
4 Crossed bones on the skirt.

Her name may be spelled logographically or logosyllabically:

  1 **CHAK CHEL**
2 **CHAK che-l(e)**

Goddess I. Within the divinatory pages of the Dresden Codex, there are many representations of a comely young goddess, seated and with bared breasts (*ill. 17*). Here are her name glyphs:

1   suffix optional   2

A number of Mayanists have identified her as the young goddess of the moon and the youthful form of Chak Chel, but this is by no means certain. Her head glyph contains the curled element in the Kaban day-sign (p. 42), and this may also be prefixed. Frequently the prefix is the color "white" (**SAK**, see **12.1.2**). Goddess I's real name has not been determined, but a **ki** postfix suggests that it ends in a **-k** sound and is probably *Ixik*, "woman."

11.4 Paired gods

Apart from the Hero Twins, other powerful pairs of gods played important roles in Maya religion. We don't understand everything about these, but the Classic period theologians liked to personify philosophical oppositions as concrete divinities – oppositions such as light vs. darkness, sky vs. earth, and so forth. The principle is embodied in the pair of aged deities who are seen paddling a canoe-load of gods on two of the bones from Jasaw Chan K'awiil's tomb at Tik'al – hence their nickname, "The Paddlers." The Paddler in front has jaguar headdress and costume details, while the aft Paddler exhibits a sting-ray spine through the septum of his nose. Their name glyphs, which are logograms representing their heads, are found on many monuments, especially those concerned with the Creation, but these may be replaced with *ak'bal* and *k'in* glyphs (in paddle-shaped cartouches), symbolizing night and day, respectively. What the names of these deities really were is yet a mystery.

 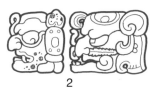

1   2   Paddler Title

11.5 Triads

The Palenque Triad consists of three gods who were born of the same divine ancestress within a three-week period in the year 2360 BC; they are known to epigraphers as GI, GII, and GIII: GI has been described in **11.3**. GII is none

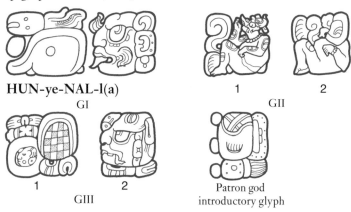

HUN-ye-NAL-l(a)
GI

1   2
GII

1   2
GIII

Patron god
introductory glyph

other than the familiar K'awiil or God K (see **11.3**), in a somewhat infantile form. However, while there has been much speculation about the identification of GIII, nothing is really known about this deity. Three other gods, probably tutelary deities like the aforementioned three, also appear together in Palenque texts:

EK'-WAY-y(a)-IB CHAAK *ek'-wayib chaak*
"Black *Way* Chaak"

GIV

God A'

GV

HUN-??-AJAW *hun-??-ajaw* "One-??-Ajaw"

GVI

Consult **11.3** for more information on Chaak and **11.6** for God A'; GVI has not yet been identified.

There are also paired and multiple gods at Tik'al and Caracol; like the Palenque Triad, they too are associated with the local polity.

11.6 The Death Gods

Within the vast corpus of Classic Maya art, there are many supernaturals connected with death and with Xibalba, the Maya Underworld, all replete with chthonic symbols (disembodied eyes, crossed bones, and the like); many of these sinister figures, however, may be *way* (see **11.7**) or spirit alter-egos of the living. Nevertheless, two death gods may be considered major members of the Maya pantheon, and will be considered here.

God A. The usual form of this deity is nothing more than an animated skeleton, and would not seem out of place on Halloween night; however, in the Dresden Codex and on some vases, the god appears as a desiccated corpse, with black "death spots" and other signs of dissolution.

God A's appellative logogram, a skull in profile with variable prefixes, is frequently found in the Dresden Codex, and is yet unreadable:

 God A glyph from the Dresden Codex

However, in the codices there are two phonetic renderings that refer to the god of death, using names or euphemisms known in the ethnohistoric sources:

 xi-b(i) *xib* "fright"
(cf. Xibalba, "Place of Fright" in the Popol Vuh)

 ki-si-n(i) *kisin* "farter" (a reference to the bad smells thought to emanate from the Maya Underworld and its denizens).

In addition, the God A glyph serves as the Head Variant for the number 10 (**LAHUN**); and for 13 through 19, the "ten" inherent in such compounds is indicated by the Death God's lower jaw.

#10   #19

God A′ One of the strangest deities in the Maya pantheon, this youthful god is usually depicted in the act of self-decapitation, cutting off his own head with a stone axe or knife. In codices and on ceramics, he is shown with the "percentage sign" [%] on his cheek, and a collar of "death eyes" – both of these elements are potent symbols of death. In the glyphs for his name, **ATAN-n(a)** the "percentage sign" may appear on the cheek, and the main sign for *ak'ab* ("darkness") in the top of the head:

1   2   3   4   5
                                                variant

11.7 The *way* spirit-companions

The existence of a vast class of supernatural beings among the Classic Maya is a recent discovery of epigraphers and iconographers, and has shed much light on both ancient society and ancient religion. First made apparent on numerous painted vases from the southern lowlands, it is now clear that these are *wayoob*, spirit-companions to the Classic elite. In many Mayan languages, the word *way* refers to a kind of spiritual double, often in animal shape, with which one remains in communion throughout life. Both the ceramic and monumental inscriptions relate a specific *way* to an individual ruler, who apparently established communion with his alter-ego in a special temple (see **12.4**) (*ill. 15*). For a thorough discussion of the concept, along with a catalogue of known *way* (complete with glyphic texts, transcriptions, and translations), see Grube and Nahm (1994).

The noun *way* is written logosyllabically, thus:

 WAY *way* "spirit-companion"

 w(a)-WAY-y(a) *way* "spirit-companion"

Wherever these weird, chimaeric creatures appear on Late Classic vases, they are usually accompanied by formulaic secondary texts that give the following:

- the name of the *way*;
- the *way* glyph prefixed by ⟨ an **u**, the 3rd person singular possessive;
- an Emblem Glyph collocation, usually meaning "the holy king of X"; or just the main sign of an Emblem Glyph. Sometimes there is only a personal name, without any Emblem Glyph at all. And, infrequently, the text simply says *u way*, without stating whose *way* it is.

Here is one such *way* text, with accompanying picture, from the beautiful and famous Altar de Sacrificios Vase:

1 **nu-pu-l(a)** *nupuul*
2 **BAHLAM-m(a)** *bahlam*
3 **u-WAY-y(a)** *u-way*
4 **K'UHUL MUTAL-l(a) AJAW**
  k'uhul mutal ajaw
  "Counterpart Jaguar, the *way* of the Holy King of Mutal (Tik'al)"

Incidentally, another of the *way* on the Altar Vase is an aspect of God A', so even some major gods, perhaps those most closely connected with death and the Underworld, may somehow be involved with the world of the spirit companions.

12

THE INANIMATE AND ANIMATE WORLDS

12.1 The physical world

The Classic Maya sense of time, so well expressed in their complex calendric notations, seems fairly unique to them. Not so with their sense of cosmological space, which they share with many other American Indian peoples, from the Pueblos and Navajos of Arizona and New Mexico down to northwestern South America. The universe was conceived by most of these as a system of seven world-directions, comprising the four cardinal points, plus the center, zenith, and nadir. On the earth's surface at each of the four directions stood a world-tree, with a specific bird atop each tree. And, finally, each cardinal point along with the center was associated with a color; the Classic Maya color-directions were as follows:

- North (*xaman*): white (*sak*)
- West (*ochk'in*): black (*ik'*)
- South (?): yellow (*k'an*)
- East (*lak'in*): red (*chak*)

These color-directions were integrated with the time dimension in a count of 819 days: in the cities of the southern lowlands during the Classic, each 819-day cycle had its own direction and appropriate color. Since some important deities like Chaak (the Rain God) and "Pawahtuun" were quadripartite, it is no surprise that in late pre-Conquest Yukatan, they too were closely associated with the color-directions.

12.1.1 *The directions*

There is still some discrepancy of opinion whether the world directions were the familiar cardinal points as we know them, or whether, as some contemporary ethnographic accounts would have it, they actually lay at the **solstice** points (the farthest north and south rising and setting points of the sun). Here we shall stick with the traditional view.

North:

 xa-m(a)-MAN-n(a) *xaman*   **xa-MAN-n(a)** *xaman*

 na?-XAMAN *na-xaman*

  **na-XAMAN** *na-xaman*

1   2

West:

 **OCH-K'IN** *ochk'in*

 OCH-K'IN-n(i) *ochk'in*

 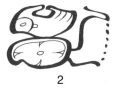 **chi-K'IN-n(i)** *chik'in* (Post-Classic spelling)

1   2

South: *Note:* although the Yukatek Maya word for "south" is *nohol*, the actual name of the direction in the inscriptions and in the codices remains unknown.

1   2   3

East:

 **LAK-K'IN** *lak'in*

Note: In these first two examples, the sound **LAK** is rendered by the rebus **LAK**, "plate." See p. 102.

 LAK-K'IN-n(i) *lak'in*

  **la-K'IN-n(i)** *lak'in*

1   2

12.1.2 *The colors*

White *(sak)*

1   2

Black *(ik')*

1   2   3

Yellow *(k'an)*

1   2

Red (*chak*) *Note:* depending on context, this glyph can be read either as *chak*, "red," or as *chak*, "great."

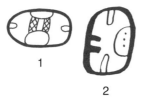

Green (*yax*) *Note:* The color is actually blue-green, Maya color terminology making no distinctions between the two. This glyph can also be read as *yax*, "first."

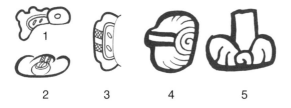

12.1.3 *The sky and the earth*

Like their Aztec cousins, the ancient Maya may have conceived of a layered heaven, consisting of 13 levels, but we have little information on this. There is but a single Maya word for "sky" or "heaven": *chan/kan*. This can be found throughout the inscriptions, in the names of gods and mortals, and elsewhere. Although the phonetic complement 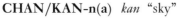 -**na** may or not be added to the logogram, there is little variation in its written form, either in the inscriptions or in the codices.

CHAN/KAN-n(a) *kan* "sky"

CHAN/KAN-n(a) *kan* "sky"

Thanks to Chaak, rain falls from the clouds in the sky onto the earth:

 MUYAL-ya-l(a) *muyal* "cloud"

 HA' *ha'* "rain", "water"

 CHAB/KAB *chab/kab* "earth"

 CHAB/KAB-b(a) *chab/kab* "earth"

To the Maya, "wind" and "breath" are the same:

   IK' *ik'* "wind," "breath"

1   2   3

The earth is not only covered with eminences, but (being karstic in nature) it is pitted with sinkholes and riddled with caves:

WITZ   **wi-WITZ**   **wi-tz(i)**   **CH'EEN**   **CH'EEN-n(a)**

witz "hill," "mountain"   *ch'een* "cave," "hollowed out place"

Water can collect on its surface, though:

    NAB *nab* "pool," "body of water"

1   2   3   4

12.2 Humans

The basic words for "human" (as opposed to "man") are *winik*, and *winal*:

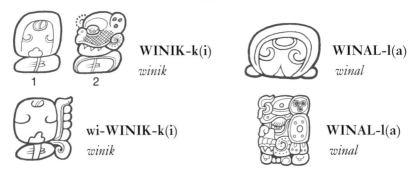

WINIK-k(i)
winik

1

2

WINAL-l(a)
winal

wi-WINIK-k(i)
winik

WINAL-l(a)
winal

"Man" in the sense of a male person is *xib*, written with the logogram **XIB** 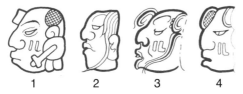; this rare glyph appears in a foursome of names assigning the god Chaak to the color-directions, as in:

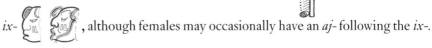

CHAK-XIB-CHAAK-k(i)
Chak-Xib-Chaak "Red Man Chaak"

In Classic Mayan, a "woman" is *ixik*, written with the logogram **IXIK** (1, 2). When prefixed, it is read as IX (3, 4).

1   2   3   4

We've already encountered agentives in **2.7.2**. To remind you, titles for male roles (offices, trades, and the like) are often prefixed by *aj-* , and female ones by *ix-* , although females may occasionally have an *aj-* following the *ix-*.

If you see a woman depicted on a monument, look for the female agentive prefix in the accompanying text – this will indicate the location of her name(s) and title(s). On the great Classic reliefs, agentives seldom appear with males.

12.3 Animals

The rich fauna of the lowland Mesoamerican tropical environment is found throughout Maya iconography and epigraphy, and even in the personal names of major Classic kings. In particular, the jaguar and its pelage acted as a potent symbol of kingly power, but many birds – especially the macaw and quetzal – were also important. A bewildering number of animals, both real and imaginary (usually chimerical), are found as names of *way* on painted Maya ceramics (see **11.7**), but we will list only those most likely to be found in Classic texts and in the codices. Here, then, is part of the Maya menagerie:

Honey bee

 KAB/CHAB-b(a) *kab/chab*

 KAB/CHAB-b(a) *kab/chab*

Fish

 **KAY/CHAY** *kay/chay*

1   2

 cha-y(a) *chay*

Snake

 **k(a)-KAN**

Note: The pronunciation is *kan* in Yukatek (and in the reading of the Palenque ruler Kan Bahlam's name), but *chan* in Ch'olti', the daughter language of Classic Ch'olti'an.

Caiman, alligator **AHIIN** *ahiin*

Turtle 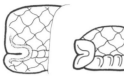 **AHK** *ahk* **a-k(u)** *ahk*

Ocellated turkey  **ku-tz'u** *kutz*

Hummingbird  **tz'u-nu-n(u)** *tz'unun*

Note: Here we have the use of two dots to indicate reduplication of the syllabogram.

 tz'u-n(u) *tz'unu(n)*

Quetzal **K'UK'** *k'uk'*

 **k'u-k'(u)** *k'uk'*

Macaw **MO'** *mo*

1 2 3 4

 **mo-o-o** *mo'*

Armadillo **i-ba-ch(a)** *ibak'* (The scribe erred here, by confusing **cha** with **k'a**.)

White-tailed deer  **CHIH** *chih*

1   2

Jaguar **BAHLAM-m(a)** *bahlam*

 ba-la-m(a) *bahlam*

Dog  **tzu-l(u)** *tzul*

Bat   **SUUTZ'** *suutz'*

1   2

Howler monkey **ba-tz'u** *baatz'*

Spider monkey  **ma-x(i)** *maax*

12.4 Buildings and structures

The world in which the ancient Maya lived was overwhelmingly a built one: just as the scribes had hieroglyphic names for all sorts of natural features in their surroundings, so they had specific terms for the artificial features of the cities within which the elite fulfilled their assigned roles. Name-tagging (see also **10.2**) is the hyphenated word epigraphers use to indicate possessed things – everything from items of personal jewelry up to huge structures. This laudable epigraphic trait enables us sometimes to discover the function of buildings that otherwise would remain a mystery.

In Classic Mayan, there are two words meaning "house," each with its own glyph. These are:

 NAAH *naah* "structure" in the general sense, whether possessed or not.

1 y(o)-**OTOOCH**-ch(u) *y-otooch*

2 y(o)-**OTOOT**-t(i) *y-otoot*

"his/her house." This word is *almost always* possessed, and thus usually takes the 3rd person singular possessive pronoun; it corresponds to the English "home" as contrasted with "house."

In the inscriptions, both of these words are used to designate specific structures within the city. Here is one such in the Palace complex at Palenque:

 **SAK**-nu-k(u)-**NAAH** *sak nuk naah* "White Pelt (?) Building"

Also at Palenque, Stephen Houston has found that each of the triad of major temples within the Cross Group, with their interior "sanctuaries," was designated as a *pibnah*, or "sweatbath," presumably where the god or the king, his earthly representative," could undertake a symbolic ritual sweating:

 pi-bi-**IL**-**NAH** *pibilnah* "sweatbath"

Some structures received the term *wayib*:

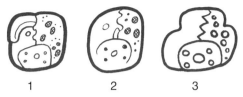

1   2   3

This could have one or more meanings. The term *way* indicates not only the spiritual alter-ego of a ruler (see **11.7**), but also the act of sleeping and/or dreaming. A *wayib* could thus be the place where the ruler could contact his *way* through dreams, or perhaps even the domicile of the *way* itself.

And, finally, *muknal*, the tomb or burial place:

In addition, there are glyphs for architectural features for which epigraphers have not yet found a Maya equivalent, such as these:

 "pyramid"

 "ballcourt" (the ball between stepped ballcourt walls).

12.5 Stone objects

The general word for stela is *lakamtuun*, "great stone," a fitting description for these often huge, inscribed monoliths with their depictions of rulers and other members of the royal house. The *lakamtuun* glyph appears on the very monument it describes:

 LAKAM-TUUN-n(i) *lakamtuun*

 la-ka-m(a)-TUUN-n(i) *lakamtuun*

The setting up of a stela was conceived by the ancient Maya as an act of planting (*tz'ap*), like the setting out of a tree:

1 tz'a-p(a) *tz'ap*
2 tz'a-p(a)-AJ *tz'apaj*
3 u-tz'a-p(a)-AW TUUN-n(i)
  tz'apaw tuun

tz'a-p(a)-AJ LAKAM-TUUN-n(i)
tz'apaj lakamtuun
"the great stone was planted"

Lintels, so important at sites like Yaxchilan and Chich'en Itza, were called *pakab*.

u-pa-ka-b(a) *u-pakab* "his/her/its lintel"
(look for this collocation on the lintels of the
Monjas building at Chich'en Itza)

The generic term for "altars," or other horizontal monuments found in front of stelae, or sometimes elsewhere, has yet to be found in the inscriptions, but at least some of these sculptures were called *k'antuun* or "yellow stone," possibly a reference to the yellowish limestone from which the best were carved:

K'AN-TUUN-n(i) *k'antuun*

Incidentally, a few stelae and altars had proper names, in addition to their generic ones, and were presumably "owned" by the rulers who had commissioned their carving and placement.

A number of censers (incense burners) of white limestone have been uncovered at Copan and, in accord with the practice of name-tagging, are carved with this glyphic collocation:

1 u-SAK-la-k(a)-TUUN-n(i)
  u-saklaktuun
  "his/her/its white stone mortar"
2 SAK-LAK-TUUN
  saklaktuun "white stone mortar"

(the Copan censers are actually mortar-shaped)

12.6 Pottery vessels

You have already encountered texts painted or carved on ceramics in Section **10.2**, where you saw that the scribes were careful to note the shape of the vessel in the Primary Standard Sequence (PSS), before giving the contents (*ill. 16*). Here, as a reminder, are the three shapes to remember:

 la-k(a) *lak* "plate" (used to hold maize tamales)

 ja-wa(n)-te *jawante* "tripod plate" (also for tamales)

 **yu-k'i-b(i)** *yuk'ib* "his vessel for drink" (a cylindrical vase for the chocolate drink)

12.7 Costume and personal adornment

In addition to their magnificent clothing, the lords and ladies depicted on Classic Maya monuments are literally loaded down with gorgeous head-dresses, feathered backracks, and jewelry carved from jade and marine shell, and you may be sure that every last item had a deeply symbolic content, and role to play in public displays and performances. The whole ensemble amounted to what was virtually an iconographic symphony of great complexity. You may also be sure that each of these costume details had its own name. Among those that we can recognize in the glyphic texts are:

 tu-pa-j(a) *tuupaj* "earspool"

 **u-tu-p(a)** *u-tuup* "his/her/its earspool"

1   2

pi-xo-m(a) *pixoom* "headcloth"

 SAK-HUUN-na *sak huun* "white headband"

 u-SAK-HUUN-AL *u-sak huunal*
"his/her/its white headband"

 u-SAK-hu-n(a)-l(a) *u-sak-huunal*
"his/her/its white headband"
(the "crown" of reigning monarchs, tied on at inauguration)

One can see the glyphs for all of these carved on the middle panel of the three great texts of the Temple of the Inscriptions at Palenque, along with this glyph depicting the shell-mosaic war helmet worn by Classic rulers.

 KO'HAW-wa *ko'haw* "helmet"

ILLUSTRATION EXAMPLES

The drawings and photographs in this section will introduce the reader to some real texts, carved, painted, or drawn on a wide variety of materials. In many cases, we have given some guidance to the general reading, but the advanced student ought to be able to work out most of these texts by him/herself. The one example from a codex (*ill. 17*) serves as a reminder that while most Maya writing was once contained in untold thousands of folding-screen books, none of this great corpus has survived except for four Post-Classic codices. Thus, our sample is skewed towards imperishable stone monuments and pottery.

1 **Lintel 24, Yaxchilan** (drawing courtesy Ian Graham).

This magnificent 8th-century lintel in the British Museum commemorates a blood-drawing ritual celebrated at night by the great Yaxchilan ruler Itzamnaaj Bahlam II ("Shield Jaguar") and his wife Lady K'abal Xook. It took place on 5 Eb 15 Mak. The text from **B1b** through **F1a** reads

u baah	"his semblance
ti ch'ahil	at the penance,
ti k'ak'al jul	with a fiery spear,
u-ch'abal kan [k'atun] *ajaw*	the penance of the 4 k'atun king
Itzamnaaj Balam	Itzamnaaj Bahlam"

The names and titles of his wife are given in **G2–G4**; she is named at **G4** as an *ix kaloomte'*, "Lady Autocrat." The sculptor's signature is given at **H3–H4**.

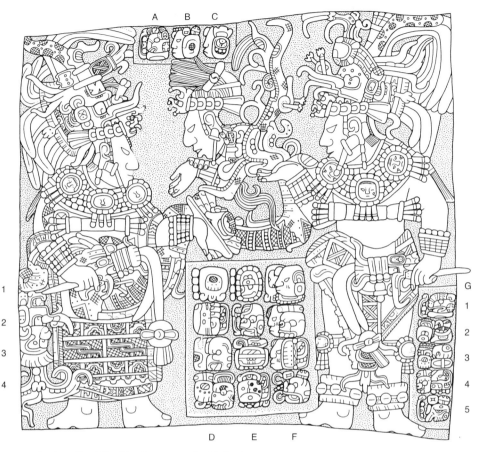

2 Lintel 14, Yaxchilan (drawing courtesy Ian Graham)

This limestone lintel is still in place, spanning one of the rooms in Temple 20. It depicts a blood-drawing rite celebrated on the Calendar Round date 4 Imix 4 Mol (9.15.10.0.0, 26 June 741) by "Great Skull," a *sajal* or war chief of the Yaxchilan kingdom, and by his sister, Lady "Great Skull," who became the wife of the king Yaxuun-Bahlam IV. The conjuring of the Vision Serpent (described as a *way* spirit in D4–E4) was carried out by the woman, not the man; her name and titles appear at B, C, and F1–F4. Following the phrase *u-bah-anul?*, "the famous?," Great Skull's full name and titles are given by G2–G5.

Note: when there are three columns in a text, the first two columns are to be read together, then the third (i.e. read D and E, then F).

3 Day glyph from Stela D, Quiriguá (photo by MDC)

Some of the calendrical inscriptions of Copan and Quiriguá are of unbelievable complexity, and were obviously to be read by only the most educated of the elite. This detail from a mid-8th-century stela shows the day sign Ajaw as the head of a crowned Hero Twin in the cartouche, with a full-figure number 7 to the left.

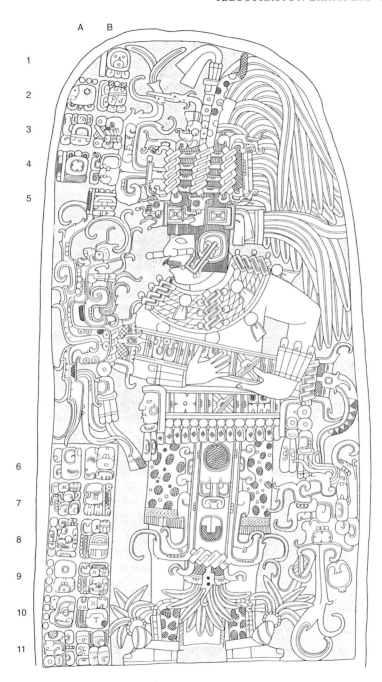

4 Stela 10, Seibal (drawing courtesy Ian Graham)

This is one of four stelae celebrating the period ending 10.1.0.0.0 (30 November 849), given by the Calendar Round date 5 Ajaw 3 K'ayab at **B1–A2**. They were erected by one Aj Bolon-? (**B5**), ruler of this enormous city on the Río Pasión, Guatemala. According to the text on the lower left, these rites were "witnessed" (*ilah*, **B7**) by important visitors from the cities of Mutal (Tik'al), **A8–B8**; Kalak'mul, **A9–B9**; and Motul de San José (?), **A10–B10**.

5 Sculptor's signature from Stela 1, Bonampak' (photo by MDC)

The expression starts with the usual *yuxul(?)*, "the carving of…," then gives the artist's name. The last two glyphs, *y-anaab* [Yaxchilan] *k'uhul ajaw*, state that he is the *aj naab* (a kind of artist) of the king of Yaxchilan, the city to which Yajaw Chan Muwaan, the lord of Bonampak', owed allegiance.

6 Arroyo de Piedra, Stela 1 (photo by MDC)

Many Classic inscriptions are badly eroded, making them difficult to read. This one, an Initial Series date from a small site in northern Guatemala, is still legible, and marks the k'atun ending 9.9.0.0.0 (at **A2–A4**) 3 Ajaw (at **B4**) 3 Sotz' (at **A5**) (9 May 613). Note the *te'* numerical classifier between the month name and its coefficient.

7 Detail from Tablet of the 96 Hieroglyphs, Palenque (photo by MDC)

Nominal glyph of the Palenque ruler K'inich K'uk' Bahlam II, who commissioned this magnificent tablet in 783. The *k'inich* title stands to the left. The "main sign" is a conflation: the head of a quetzal (*k'uk'*) appears with the ear of a jaguar (*bahlam*).

8 Detail of platform inscription from Temple XIX, Palenque (photo by MDC)

Part of a very long, recently discovered text of 220 glyphs that is still being deciphered. The lightly incised glyphs are beautifully drawn, and relate the accession of Palenque ruler K'inich Ahkal Mo' Naab III to the birth of the city's ancestral gods. In this view, we can see the Calendar Round date 13 Kimi 19 Keh at A3–B3, and Distance Numbers at C4–D4 and E3–E4. Birth glyphs at A2, A4, and C1 are followed by the names of deities (GIII of the Palenque Triad appears at B4).

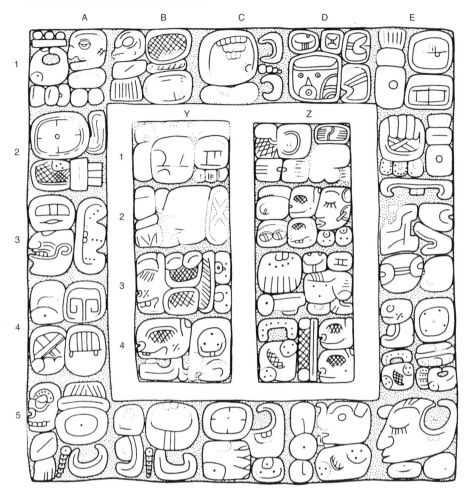

9 Lintel 4, Las Monjas, Chich'en Itza (drawing courtesy Ian Graham)

Most of Chich'en's inscriptions appear on lintels in the Las Monjas ("Nunnery") complex, and are of great interest for their high degree of syllabic writing, and for the names of Maya leaders and families known from the post-Conquest annals. The dedication of Lintel 4 and its carving are given by B5–E5. Named at Y3 is K'ak'upakal, mentioned in Colonial-period texts as a brave Itza war leader. The protagonist is to be found at Z4: *k'uhul aj k'ak'*, "the holy one of fire."

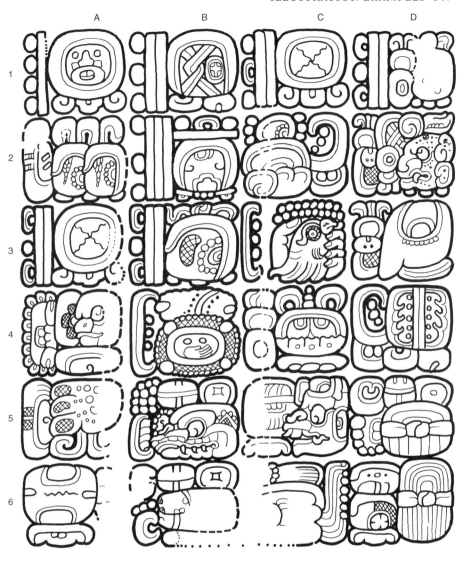

10 Inscription on wooden lintel, Temple I, Tik'al (drawing by MVS)

Many Maya inscriptions must have been carved in wood, but only a few have survived. Here is what the first part of this text says:

A1–B1	9 Ajaw 13 Pop (9.13.3.0.0) [28 February 695]
B2	[count forward] 18 k'ins and 7 winals [to]
A3–B3	11 Etz'nab 11 Ch'en (9.13.3.7.18) [5 August 695]
A4–B4	*jubuy u-took' pakal* "his flint [and] shield get knocked down,"
A5	*yich'aak k'ak'* Yich'aak K'ak' ("Fiery Claw"),
B5	*k'uhul Kan ajaw* "holy lord of Kan (Kalak'mul)"

This commemorates an important victory over Kalak'mul by the great Tik'al king Jasaw Chan K'awiil I, whose name is given at D4–C5.

11 **Stucco glyphs from Temple XIX, Palenque** (photo by MVS)

There must have been many stucco inscriptions on and in Maya buildings, especially on roof combs, but surviving ones are rare. Although the coefficient numbers are damaged, this polychromed glyph block records a Calendar Round date, 7 Ajaw 13 Muwan. (9.14.0.0.0, or AD 711).

12 Engraved bones from Burial 196, Tik'al (photo by MVS)

Each of these tools (possibly awls for working baskets or weaving pins) has a name-tagging text. Both begin with the phrase *u-baak*, "the bone of…." The owner of the left-hand bone is given only as "the Holy Lord of Mutal (Tik'al)," while the one on the right reads *a-chak-?-te*, a known but yet-undeciphered title borne by the Tik'al ruler Yik'in (?) Chan K'awiil. The scribe has filled the lines with red hematite for legibility.

13 Naj Tunich Cave, Drawing 52 (photo courtesy Andrea Stone)

This is one of a large number of painted inscriptions left by ancient scribes and pilgrims on the walls of Naj Tunich, an immense cavern near the Guatemala-Belize border. The 8th-century text contains two Calendar Round dates (1 Men 13 Pax at A1–B1, and 3 Ajaw 3 Mol at A3–B3), separated by a Distance Number. The event is the "arrival" (*huli*, at A4) of a personage described as a "foreign artist(?)" (*tzul y-anaab* at A7–B7).

14 Painted vase in Nak'be style (photo by MDC)

Some of the most talented Classic scribes both wrote texts and painted scenes upon the surfaces of elite
ceramics. Below the rim of this unprovenanced vase from northern Guatemala, appears a Primary Standard
sequence or PSS, beginning with the Initial Sign at the left. The text ends on the other side with the name
and titles of the owner or patron.

15 Detail from the Altar de Sacrificios Vase (photo by MDC)

This small 8th-century vase from a burial at the site of Altar de Sacrificios on the Río Pasión in northern Guatemala can be counted as one of the supreme masterpieces of Classic Maya art. In this detail, an aged supernatural or *way* dances with a snake, and partly obscures the PSS in the rim band above. The second glyph to the right of his hand reads *kakaw* or "chocolate," which the vase once held. The remaining secondary texts identify the various *wayoob* on the pot, and name their royal "owners."

16 The "Resurrection Plate" (photo courtesy Justin Kerr)

This famous plate is in "codex style," and shows the resurrection from the earth (depicted as a turtle carapace) of the Maize God by his two sons, the Hero Twins. The first two glyphs in the rim band form the dedication section of the PSS. The fourth glyph reads *u-lak*, "the plate of...," and the final three glyphs give the name of the owner or patron. Each of the actors in this drama faces his own name glyph.

17 Omen texts in the Dresden Codex (after Förstemann 1880)

This is the bottom third of page 16 of the Dresden Codex, probably painted in the 14th or 15th century, but copying much earlier material. Painted with brush and quill pens, this detail shows part of a 5 x 52-day divinatory almanac relating to a young Goddess I (possibly named *Ixik*) and the bird omens associated with her. The name of each bird appears in the first glyph of the four-glyph block above each seated figure, followed by the phrase *u-muut* "the omen of…", her name, and the augury for good or ill. The *k'uk'*, "quetzal," and *mo-o-o*, "macaw" glyphs (see **12.3**) gave Y.V. Knorosov important clues for his decipherment of Maya writing.

SYLLABARY

Maya writing is not nearly as standardized as we have come to expect a modern writing system to be: Maya scribes expressed enormous creativity in their forms of each sign, so that the style of drawing a "jaguar" or a "sky" glyph, for instance, changes not only from one site to another, but sometimes even within a single text. In our Syllabary and Lexicon , we have chosen one, or more often two or three, relatively "standard" examples, but we have often tried to illustrate somewhat different forms elsewhere in the book, with the intention of allowing the reader to discover for him or herself the commonalities between this or that "jaguar" and this or that "sky," in as many contexts as possible. Once one begins to conceive of this "inconsistency" as an asset rather than a liability, one can begin to enjoy and appreciate the extraordinary vitality of the artists and scribes who produced this sumptuous writing.

The problem of devising an effective writing system has been solved many times, to fit many languages. In virtually every case, the solution has involved a combination of *logographic* signs (such as our numerals and those other signs found on the margins of our typewriter keyboards) and *phonetic* signs. The Maya were no different; in a given text you might expect to find 40–50 percent of the signs to be phonetic.

Technically speaking, every Maya syllabic sign represents a consonant plus a vowel, or CV. Most speakers of English and other European languages, however, do not distinguish the glottal stop consonant, so you would read the signs in the first column as if they were pure (Spanish) vowels. (Americans encounter the glottal stop represented as an apostrophe in Hawaiian words like Hawai'i, where the stop is the brief silence between the two i's. In Britain, Cockney dialect replaces some intervocalic t's with the glottal stop: "bottle of water" becomes "bo'le of wa'er.")

The value of the signs in each cell in the grid corresponds to the sum of the consonant along the top and the vowel in the left margin. Thus, a glyph in column "ch'" and in row "o" reads *ch'o*.

The blanks in this table represent syllables for which no one has convincingly discovered a sign – yet. Some of these signs also had a logographic reading (sometimes completely different from the syllabic reading), and one or two may have had two different syllabic readings. (For example, the 'bat-head' signs under *xu* and *tz'i* appear almost identical, but they may well have had distinct features that became blurred as time went on and close comparison may yet detect what these were.) In other cells there may be two or several signs. This reflects the large vocabulary of alternative signs from which the Maya scribes could choose. Apparently they valued visual variety highly, the same way writers the world over strive to use various synonyms to avoid repetition. (This is also true of traditional Japanese poetry; though the official Japanese syllabary has only some 50 distinct signs, there exist dozens of alternate forms one can use to enrich the visual texture.) Some of the examples we have chosen are simply two versions of the same sign, to show the wide tolerance these signs enjoyed in formal variations. Other alternate forms are utterly different from each other. We have striven to select the clearest examples, while indicating the breadth of form you will encounter.

Ever since the reevaluation of Landa's "alphabet" and Knorosov's first proposed phonetic readings, many epigraphers have collected the known Maya syllabograms into tidy tables like this one. Between about 1970 and about 1990, the cells in the Syllabary filled up one by one, some with very secure readings and some merely attractive suggestions. As epigraphers have sharpened their understanding of the Maya writing system, they have reassigned several glyphs once thought to be syllabic (such as **TE'** and **K'UH**) as logograms, and other proposed signs have simply fallen by the wayside. In this table we have tried to be conservative, including only signs for which readings are unassailable. Even so, some we inserted hesitantly, appending a question mark against the possibility that these may some day be reassigned.

As explained in Chapter 2, a syllabic glyph at the end of a word root behaves very differently from the simple CV signs we find elsewhere. Its vowel usually becomes silent, and it functions as if it were a pure consonant. Or it may function semi-logographically as a *morphosyllable*, and "reverse" its pronunciation to a VC; thus **ja** would read **-AJ**, **li** as **-IL**, etc.

pure vowels	b	ch	ch'	h

	j	k	k'	l	m
a					
e					
i					?
o					
u					

n	p	s	t	t'

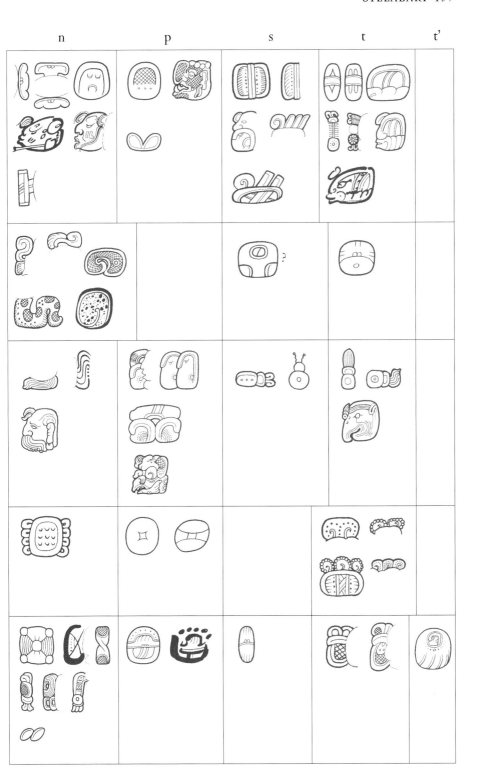

	tz	tz'	w	x	y
a					
e					
i					
o					
u					

A MAYA LEXICON

Most epigraphers today draw a firm distinction between logograms and syllabograms, but it is increasingly clear that the ancient Maya perceived the two categories of signs rather more fluidly. Because the spoken language was loaded with homonyms (such as *chak*, which can mean either "red" or "great"), they employed many logographic signs as rebuses, for example using the "hand" sign **CH'AM** not only for the obvious "grasp," but also for its homonym **CH'AM** "oversee." They likewise used the "bone" sign for **BAAK**, "bone," and also for **BAAK** "captive," and in the Terminal Classic period began to interchange the signs for "snake," "sky," or "4," all of which read **CHAN**, even going so far as to use the "snake head" for a near-homonym **CHAAN**, "possession." Multiple interpretations such as these we have separated by a forward slash /.

A number of logographic signs also acted as syllabograms. Some had completely different syllabic readings. The most salient example is the "stone" sign for **TUUN**, which as a syllable reads **ku**. Many others appear as *acrophonic* syllables, where the phonetic value is simply the initial part of the logographic reading. Examples: **BIH** "road," which frequently does duty as the syllable **bi**. We again have indicated these doubled readings with a forward slash /. There are also the "reversible" *morphosyllables* that behave as both logograms and syllabograms at once. These you will find in the Syllabary chart.

Technically, most Maya word-roots take the form CVC; that is, consonant-vowel-consonant, though a few words, such as *bolon* "nine" are CVCVC. However, to find a root by itself is relatively rare. Spoken Maya, like spoken English, is full of words that consist of root-plus-affixes (either prefix or suffix); these are usually more common than any root alone. The word "capture," for instance, almost never appears by itself; "he is captured" is the way we see it in the inscriptions. Many other important words tend to be spelled phonetically. Thus we found it helpful to include in this list the commonest *collocations* – groups of glyphs that are often found together – rather than try strictly to limit it to "pure" logograms.

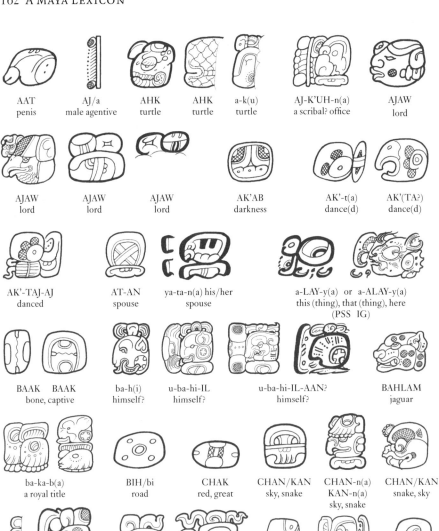

AAT
penis

AJ/a
male agentive

AHK
turtle

AHK
turtle

a-k(u)
turtle

AJ-K'UH-n(a)
a scribal? office

AJAW
lord

AJAW
lord

AJAW
lord

AJAW
lord

AK'AB
darkness

AK'-t(a)
dance(d)

AK'(TA?)
dance(d)

AK'-TAJ-AJ
danced

AT-AN
spouse

ya-ta-n(a) his/her
spouse

a-LAY-y(a)   or   a-ALAY-y(a)
this (thing), that (thing), here
(PSS IG)

BAAK   BAAK
bone, captive

ba-h(i)
himself?

u-ba-hi-IL
himself?

u-ba-hi-IL-AAN?
himself?

BAHLAM
jaguar

ba-ka-b(a)
a royal title

BIH/bi
road

CHAK
red, great

CHAN/KAN
sky, snake

CHAN-n(a)
KAN-n(a)
sky, snake

CHAN/KAN
snake, sky

CHAN   u-cha?-CHAAN-n(u)
4, sky,   his captive/his property
snake

?
child of father

?

CHOK
scatter

chu-ka-AJ
captured

CHUM-m(u)
be seated

CHUM?-AJAW
sit as *Ajaw*

CHUM-
TUUN-n(i)
stone-seating

CH'AB
fast, penance

ch'a-ho-m(a)

ch'a-ho-m(a)
a royal title

CH'AM/
K'AM
grasp

CH'AM/
K'AM-
K'AWIIL
grasp the
K'awiil
scepter

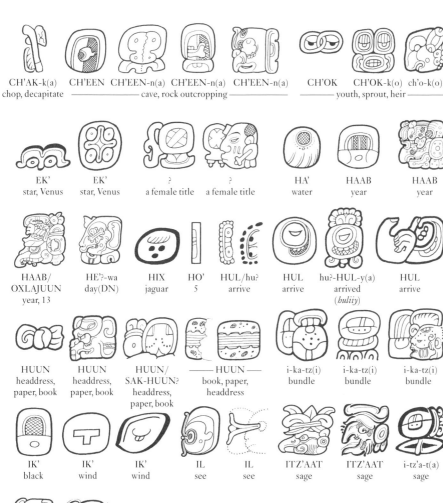

CH'AK-k(a)
chop, decapitate

CH'EEN

CH'EEN-n(a)

CH'EEN-n(a)

CH'EEN-n(a)

cave, rock outcropping

CH'OK

CH'OK-k(o)

ch'o-k(o)

youth, sprout, heir

EK'
star, Venus

EK'
star, Venus

?
a female title

?
a female title

HA'
water

HAAB
year

HAAB
year

HAAB/
OXLAJUUN
year, 13

HE'?-wa
day(DN)

HIX
jaguar

HO'
5

HUL/hu?
arrive

HUL
arrive

hu?-HUL-y(a)
arrived
(*huliy*)

HUL
arrive

HUUN
headdress,
paper, book

HUUN
headdress,
paper, book

HUUN/
SAK-HUUN?
headdress,
paper, book

——HUUN——
book, paper,
headdress

i-ka-tz(i)
bundle

i-ka-tz(i)
bundle

i-ka-tz(i)
bundle

IK'
black

IK'
wind

IK'
wind

IL
see

IL
see

ITZ'AAT
sage

ITZ'AAT
sage

i-tz'a-t(a)
sage

IXIK-k(i)
woman

IX-/na-
Lady, woman

JAL
creation verb

JANAHB
a flower

JAPAY?/WAY?
maw, portal
to the
Underworld

-ji-y(a)
-ed (past verb
ending)

JOL
head, skull

JOY/HOK?
accession
verb

JOY/HOK?
accession
verb

JUL
pierce

HUN
one

u-HUN-TAN-n(a)
her cherished one
(= her child)

KA'
2

KAB/CHAB
Earth

KAB/CHAB
Earth

?-ka-ka-w(a)
cacao

ka-ka-w(a)
cacao

KALOOM -m(a)-TE'
a royal war title

KALOOM -TE'
a royal war title

ka-lo-m(a) -TE'
a royal war title

k(a)-KAN
snake, sky

KO'HAW-w(a)
helmet,
headdress

ku-ch(u)
burden

K'ABA
name

CH'OK-K'ABA
youth name

K'AK'
fire

K'AK'
fire

K'AK'
fire

K'AL
tie, close

K'AL?
20

K'AL?
20

K'AN
yellow, precious

"K'atun"
20 Tuuns

"K'atun"
20 Tuuns

"K'atun"
20 Tuuns

K'AWIIL
K'awiil, "God
K"

K'AWIIL-l(a)
K'awiil,
"God K"

K'AWIIL
K'awiil,
"God K"

K'IN
day, sun

K'IN/K'INICH
day, sun, 4

K'INICH
a royal
title

K'INICH
a royal
title

K'INICH-K'IN-
n(i)-ch(i)
a royal title

———— K'UH/K'UHUL ————
god, holy, sacred

K'UK'
quetzal

k'u-k'(u)
quetzal

-la-j(a)
antipassive
ending

la-k(a)
plate

LAKAM
big

LAKAM-TUUN-n(i)
big stone (= stela)

la-ka-m(a)-TUUN-n(i)
big stone (= stela)

MAM

ma-m(a)
———— grandfather, ancestor ————

MO'   MO'   MO'   MO'
———————————— macaw ————————————

mu-ka-AJ
is buried

MUYAL
cloud

-na-j(a)?
passive verb ending?

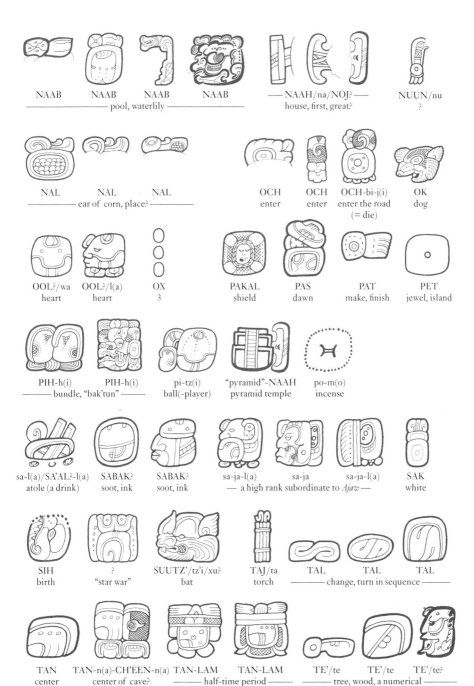

NAAB NAAB NAAB NAAB — NAAH/na/NOJ? — NUUN/nu
———————— pool, waterlily ———————— house, first, great? ?

NAL NAL NAL OCH OCH OCH-bi-j(i) OK
———— ear of corn, place? ———— enter enter enter the road dog
(= die)

OOL?/wa OOL?/l(a) OX PAKAL PAS PAT PET
heart heart 3 shield dawn make, finish jewel, island

PIH-h(i) PIH-h(i) pi-tz(i) "pyramid"-NAAH po-m(o)
—— bundle, "bak'tun" —— ball(-player) pyramid temple incense

sa-l(a)/SA'AL?-l(a) SABAK? SABAK? sa-ja-l(a) sa-ja sa-ja-l(a) SAK
atole (a drink) soot, ink soot, ink — a high rank subordinate to *Ajaw* — white

SIH ? SUUTZ'/tz'i/xu? TAJ/ta TAL TAL TAL
birth "star war" bat torch ———— change, turn in sequence ————

TAN TAN-n(a)-CH'EEN-n(a) TAN-LAM TAN-LAM TE'/te TE'/te TE'/te?
center center of cave? ———— half-time period ———— ———— tree, wood, a numerical ————
(usually half-K'atun) classifier

TI? — mouth?

TOOK' — flint

TOOK' — flint

TOOK'-PAKAL-l(a) — flint & shield (an emblem of war)

u-to-k'(a)-(u)-pa-ka-l(a) — his flint & (his) shield

TUUN-n(i) — stone

TUUN-n(i)-AJAW — stone lord

T'ABAY-y(i) —— ascend, raise, exalt, finish ——

T'ABAY-y(i)

u-TZAK-AW — s/he conjured

TZAM? — throne

TZAM? — throne

tzi-k(a)-HAAB-? — count of years?

tzu-k(u) — partition

TZUTZ — to end

TZUTZ — to end

u-TZ'AK-AJ —— it changed, it followed ——

u-TZ'AK-AJ

tz'a-p(a) — (to) plant

tz'a-pa-AJ — planted

tz'i-b(a) — write, paint

u-tz'i-b(i) — his writing, painting

u-h(a)-AJ — it is the jewel, necklace

u-l(u) — white atole (a drink)

WAK WAK — 6, raised

-wa-n(i) — positional verb suffix

WAY   WAY   WAY —— spirit alter-ego ——

WAY-IB — dreaming place

WINIK/WINAL

wi-WINIK-k(i) —— person, "month" ——

WINAL-l(a)

WITZ — mountain, hill

y(a)-YAL-l(a) —— child of mother ——

y(a)-YAL-l(a)

y(a)-YAL-l(a) K'UHUL-IXIK — child of divine woman

YAX   YAX   YAX —— green, blue ——

yi-ch(i)-NAL-l(a) — witness?, companion?

YOP/yo — leaf

YOP-AAT-t(a) — a deity

YOPAAT — a deity

y(o)-OTOOT —— his/her house ——

y(o)-OTOOT-t(i)

yu-k'i?-bi-IL —— his/her drinking vessel ——

yu-k'i?-bi-IL

yu-xu?-l(u) — his/her carving

CALENDRICAL FORMULAE
AND TABLES

Long Count to Julian Calendar dates

As explained in **3.3**, Maya scholars generally write out Long Count dates in a pseudo-decimal system. Thus, a Long Count of 9 bak'tuns, 15 k'atuns, 0 tuns, 0 winals, and 0 k'ins is written 9.15.0.0.0. How does one convert this to a day in the Julian system? All such calculations depend on the correct correlation between the Maya and Christian calendars. Each competing correlation that has been suggested by one specialist or another proposes a **correlation constant**, the number that is to be added to the total number of days in a specific Long Count date to reach the **Julian Day** (this has nothing to do with the Julian Calendar, but is a day-to-day count used by astronomers in place of our own cumbersome calendar). Most modern Mayanists use a constant of 584,285. Each Julian Day has its Julian or Gregorian Calendar equivalent. Thus, by adding this to the day total for 9.15.0.0.0, one reaches the Julian Day of 1988285, which equals 18 August AD 731. The late Linda Schele taught her many students to use the following formula for such a calculation, which requires only an inexpensive, handheld calculator.

1   Find the total number of days in the Long Count (LC) by the following method:
    (bak'tun coeff. x 144,000) + (k'atun coeff. x 7,200) + (tun coeff. x 360) + (winal coeff. x 20)
    + k'in coeff. = LC day total
2   Add 584,285 to the LC total and divide by 365.25, then subtract 4712. The integer (to the left of the decimal) is the Julian Calendar year.
3   Multiply 365.25 by the decimal remainder in (2), and round upward.
4   You will now have a number between 1 and 366. Find the nearest number in the table below, which will indicate the Julian month. Subtract this number from the rounded result in (3); this will give the day of that month.

Table

Jan	0	May	120	Sep	243
Feb	31	Jun	151	Oct	273
Mar	59	Jul	181	Nov	304
Apr	90	Aug	212	Dec	334

Example: 9.9.2.4.8 = 1,361,608 + 584,285 = 1,945,893 ÷ 365.25 = 5327.5646 - 4712 = 615.5646
365.25 x .5646 = 206.22015 = 207 - 181 = 26 or 26 July AD 615 (this is 29 July AD 615, Gregorian).

The Lord of the Night (Glyph G)

Since the Lord of the Night on 4 Ajaw 8 Kumk'u (the start of our era) is G9, and 360 is evenly divisible by 9, all tun endings are G9, and only the winal and k'in positions need to be calculated. Find the total number of days in these two units, and divide by 9; the remainder is the G.

SOFTWARE PROGRAMS

There are several available software programs that can make the otherwise onerous task of calculating Maya (and Gregorian) dates relatively quick and easy, doing away with the use of the bulky tables that are necessary when figuring out Calendar Rounds from Long Counts, and vice versa, the traditional way. With the advent of palm or handheld computers, with high memory capacities, it should be possible to use these programs to calculate Maya dates while "in the field" at such sites as Copan and Tik'al. Here are two currently available programs:

Iwal Ut © 1996-7 by Shawn M. Brisbin. Version 3.03 for use with DOS or Windows. Last updated in April 1999, this program can be downloaded from **http://www.xibalba.com/clients/iwalut/index.html**. With it, one can calculate the Lord of the Night, the Moon Age, and the position in the 819-day Count, as well as the more usual conversions between Long Count and Calendar Round, and between Long Count and the Julian or Gregorian Calendars. One can also reckon "Old Era" dates (in the last Great Cycle, prior to the 4 Ajaw 8 Kumk'u Creation).

Maya Calendar © Gregory Reddick. Version 2.02. Available as a download from **http://www.xoc.net**. This easy-to-use software gives you a stylized picture of an Initial Series corresponding to a specific Long Count date, as it might appear on a Maya stela. Also included in this program are calculations for the Lord of the Night, Old Era dates, the 819-day Count (including associated colors and directions), and the Moon Age. As with Iwal Ut, one can change between rival correlation constants (although 584,285 remains the default). It takes just a few seconds to find what one's birth date would look like on a Classic stone monument!

EXERCISE ANSWERS

EXERCISE 1 (page 22)

1 mo-o-o
2 chu-ka-j(a)
3 mu-ka-j(a)
4 ba-ka-b(a)
5 tu-p(a)
6 pa-ka-l(a)
7 tz'i-b(i)
8 ch'o-k(o)

EXERCISE 2 (page 45)

6 Ak'bal 11 Ch'en
13 Ix 2 Mol
10 Kawak 17 Mak
3 Imix 9 Yax
8 Ik' 0 Pop

EXERCISE 3 (page 49)

9.12.2.0.16   5 Kib 14 Yaxk'in

EXERCISE 4 (page 55)

Distance Number 1.3.8 (8 tuns, 3 winals, 1 k'in) *uutiiy* ("it happened [on]")
1 Kawak 12 Sak. *Note*: this Distance Number is to be *subtracted* from the date that
precedes it.

EXERCISE 5 (page 57)

A1–B1	8.19.10.10.17	5 Kaban 15 Yaxk'in
B3–A4	8.19.10.11.0	8 Ajaw 18 Yaxk'in
A6–B6	+ 7.13	
C1–D1	8.19.11.0.13	5 Ben 11 Muwan
C6	17 k'atuns	
D6–E1	9.17.5.0.0	6 Ajaw 13 K'ayab
E5–F5	+ 3.4	
E6	9.17.5.3.4	5 K'an 12 Wo

As you can see, there are no Distance Numbers connecting the first and second,
and the third and fourth, of these dates. The first date marks the arrival in AD 426
of K'inich Yax K'uk' Mo', the founder of Copan's ruling dynasty, at his accession
place. A "17 k'atun" notation serves to throw the narrative into the 8th century.
The final date commemorates the dedication of the altar itself in AD 776 by Yax
Pasaj Chan Yoat, the 16th king.

EXERCISE 6 (page 58)

A1–B1	Introductory glyph
A2–B2	9 bak'tuns, 15 k'atuns
A3–B3	10 tuns, 0 winals,

A4–B4	0 k'ins	3 Ajaw
A5–B5	G9+F	9D (= 9 days)
A6–B6	3C	X4
A7–B7	B	10A (= 30 days)
A8	3 Mol	

This is the Initial Series date 9.15.10.0.0 3 Ajaw 3 Mol (26 June 741). The Supplementary Series between the day and month signs is to be read as follows:
G9 (Ninth Lord of the Night) (elided with a truncated version of Glyph F)
9E+D (29 days have elapsed since the last New Moon)
3C (the third in a cycle of six consecutive lunations)
X (the unknown god presiding over this particular lunation)
B (*u ch'ok k'aba*, "his princely name")
10A (this lunation has 30 days)

EXERCISE 7 (page 85)

1   The protagonist is "Bird Jaguar IV," ruler of Yaxchilan. He has taken 20 captives, and is a "3 K'atun Ajaw" (that is, between 40 and 60 years of age). On the actual sculpture (Lintel 29), he is described as performing a conjuring rite – in this case, conjuring up the royal lineage god K'awiil from a double-headed snake.

2   The lord is Jasaw Chan K'awiil, "Holy Lord of Mutal (Tik'al)" (B3–C1) and a *kaloomte'* (C4). The Calendar Round (A1–A2) at the top of the upper vertical panel is 6 Ajaw 13 Muwan, corresponding to the Long Count position 9.14.0.0.0, or 1 December 711 (see the formula given above for calculating Julian from Long Count dates). Here on Stela 16 this great king, who is described as a "3 K'atun Lord" and a *kaloomte'* on the lower right panel, is celebrating a Period Ending rite, the completion of the 14th k'atun of the 9th bak'tun (A3–A4). Incidentally, Jasaw Chan K'awiil is the man entombed beneath Temple I, in whose honor this structure was raised.

EXERCISE 8 (page 92)

This famous relief shows two warriors, each grasping a captive. The primary text is found at the upper left and upper right of the lintel, and reads thus:

A1–A2	7 Imix 14 Sek	
A3	**chu-ka-AJ** *chuhkaj* "is captured"	
A4	**u-"Jeweled Skull"** (a modern nickname)	
E1	**u-ba-k(i)** *u-baak* "the captive of"	
E2	**ya-YAXUUN-BAHLAM** *yaxuun-bahlam*	
E3	**K'UHUL-?-AJAW** *k'uhul-?-ajaw* "Holy King of Yaxchilan"	

"Jeweled Skull"'s name glyph is on the thigh of the right-hand captive.

The text in the middle reads:

B1	**u-CHA'AN** *u-cha'an* "he is the master of"
C1	**ko-TE'-AJAW** *ko-te'-ajaw* (the name of the second captive)
D1	**K'AN-n(a)-to-k(o)** *k'an-tok* K'an Tok
D2	**WAY-IB** (second part of name)
D3	**sa-ja-l(a)** *sajal* "sajal" (title of war leader or provincial governor)

Accordingly, the text says that Yaxuun Bahlam IV, the king of Yaxchilan, and his *sajal* K'an Tok Wayib captured Jeweled Skull and another enemy called Kote' Ajaw on 7 Imix 14 Sek (9.16.4.1.1, or 5 May 755).

EXERCISE 9 (page 93)

A1–B1	9.13. 9.14.15	7 Men 18 K'ank'in
C1–C3	+ 1. 8. 6.18	
E1–D1	9.14.18. 3.13	7 Ben 16 K'ank'in
F3–G1	+ 1.14. 7	
H1–G2	9.15. 0. 0. 0	4 Ajaw 13 Yax
I2–J1	+ 1. 0. 0.0	
J2–K2	9.16. 0. 0. 0	2 Ajaw 13 Sek

Note: the glyphs at D1 and K1 read *i-pas*, "forward to dawn." The Piedras Negras Emblem Glyph appears at F2, I1, and L3.

Date 1: Ruler 4 is born (on 18 November 701). After his name, his title, *Ch'ok* ("Prince"), is given at B3.

Date 2: Ruler 4 accedes to the throne, six days short of his 28th birthday. He now has the title of *K'uhul Ajaw* of Piedras Negras. Date 3: Celebration of the 15th Katun (see H2–G3) by Ruler 4.

Date 4: Celebration of the 16th Katun (see J3–L1) by Ruler 4. This fell on 5 May 751.

EXERCISE 10 (page 107)

A through E make up the vessel dedication phrase; note the Initial Sign at A, and the head of "Pawahtuun" at C. D reads **tz'i-b(i)**, *tz'ib*, "writing," using a head variant of the **bi** syllabogram. The vase and its contents are given by F–H. At F is the "vessel for drink" glyph, identifying this vase as one used to hold a liquid beverage. The beverage appears at H, underspelled as **ka-w(a)**; this should be **ka-ka-w(a)**, *kakaw*, "chocolate." The **SAK-yu-t(a)** preceding it may describe a kind of chocolate. The owner or patron of the vase is given at I–L. It is a woman of queenly rank, entitled **IX-MUTAL-(la) AJAW**, *Ix Mutal Ajaw*, she is probably from Tik'al rather than Dos Pilas. The final glyph names her as a *Bakab*.

BRIEF BIBLIOGRAPHY

Those wishing to see and use Maya hieroglyphic texts should examine these two major sources, one covering the inscriptions in line drawings and photographs, and the other presenting photographic rollouts of Classic Maya ceramics. Both are indispensable.

- *Corpus of Maya Hieroglyphic Inscriptions.* Issued since 1955 by the Peabody Museum, Harvard University, under the direction of Ian Graham.
- *The Maya Vase Book.* Issued since 1989 by Justin and Barbara Kerr, New York. Six volumes have appeared so far; these include essays by many leading Mayanists.

A number of important epigraphic articles have appeared in *Research Reports on Ancient Maya Writing,* with 44 numbers issued since 1985. These may be ordered from: Center for Maya Research, Post Office Box 65760, Washington, D.C. 20035-5760

Every year since 1977, there has been a Maya Hieroglyphic Workshop at the University of Texas in Austin, presided over by Linda Schele until her untimely death in 1998. The workbooks for these sessions presented the latest thinking by her and other leading scholars on the decipherment, and introduced thousands to the subject. Especially recommended is the *Notebook for the XXIIIrd Maya Hieroglyphic Forum at Texas* (1999), with an extremely important contribution by David Stuart, Stephen Houston, and John Robertson on the "Classic Mayan" (i.e. Classic Ch'olti'an) language. This and past notebooks are available from: Maya Meetings, Post Office Box 3500, Austin, TX 78764-3500

Coe, Michael D. *Breaking the Maya Code*, Revised edition. New York 1999. (Popular account of the Maya decipherment.)

——————, *The Maya.* 7th edition. London and New York 2005.

Drew, David. *The Lost Chronicles of the Maya Kings.* Berkeley and Los Angeles 2000.

Grube, Nikolai and Werner Nahm. "A census of Xibalba: a complete inventory of *Way* characters on Maya ceramics." In *The Maya Vase Book*, Volume 4: 686–715. New York 1994.

Harris, John F. and Stephen K. Stearns. *Understanding Maya Inscriptions: a Hieroglyphic Handbook.* 2nd revised edition. Philadelphia 1997. (Much more detailed than the present volume, this introduction is especially important for its coverage of Maya calendrics and astronomy, and for its exhaustive bibliography. However, many of the non-calendric readings need updating.)

Martin, Simon and Nikolai Grube. *Chronicle of the Maya Kings and Queens.* London and New York 2000. (A complete and beautifully illustrated history of the Classic kingdoms, informed by the latest advances in Maya decipherment; the hieroglyphs and dates for many more rulers are given than we present in our book.)

Maudslay, Alfred P. *Biologia Centrali-Americana, Archaeology.* Text and 4 vols. of plates.

London 1889-1902. (The forerunner of the Harvard *Corpus*, these large-format volumes contain magnificent photographs and meticulous drawings of Maya monuments. Facsimile edition 1974 by Dr. Francis Robicsek, Charlotte, North Carolina.)

Sharer, Robert J. *The Ancient Maya*. 5th edition. Stanford 1994.

Stuart, David. "Ten Phonetic Syllables," *Research Reports on Ancient Maya Writing*, 14. Washington 1987 (A pioneering work in ascribing phonetic values to Maya syllabograms, and a case study in how modern decipherment is actually carried out.)

Stuart, David, and Stephen Houston. *Classic Maya Place Names*. Washington 1987.

Thompson, J. Eric S. *A Catalog of Maya Hieroglyphs*. Norman 1962. (Covers glyphs of both the monuments and codices. While it is seriously in need of revision, many epigraphers still use its system of "T-numbers" to refer to individual glyphs.)

————, *Maya Hieroglyphic Writing An Introduction*. 3rd edition. Norman 1971. (A monumental survey by one of the great Mayanists of the last century, but now seriously out-of-date, and misleading about the nature of Maya writing. Nevertheless, extremely useful for its coverage of Maya calendrics, astronomy, and iconography.)

Villacorta, J. Antonio and Carlos A. *Códices mayas*. Guatemala 1930. (Reproduces the Dresden, Madrid, and Paris codices in remarkably accurate and useful drawings. This edition has been reprinted several times in Guatemala.)

ACKNOWLEDGMENTS

We would like to thank David Stuart, Nikolai Grube, Robert Wald, Barbara MacLeod, and many other glyph colleagues who unstintingly offered advice and suggestions throughout the process of writing this book. We owe a very special debt to the kindness and patience of Stephen Houston and Simon Martin, who vetted every section, and who answered so many of our questions. Although there is broad agreement on the decipherment, this is an area that is still in a degree of intellectual flux, and none of our friends should be held responsible for any errors that we may have committed during our search for the solution to certain problems. Mark is also grateful to his daughter Caroline and his wife Janis, and especially to the continuing support of his parents Jim and Ruth.

INDEX

Page numbers in *italic* refer to the Illustration Examples

accession, of a ruler 61
adjectives 27, 31
agentive: nouns 28–29;
  pronoun/prefix 75, 77, 79,
  128
Ajaw, glyphic forms 75
allograms 20
Altar de Sacrificios Vase 122,
  152
altars 134; Copan 57;
  Piedras Negras 93
animal glyphs 129–31, *144*
anniversaries 56
Arroyo de Piedra, Stela I *143*
artists *see* scribes and artists
aspirates 9, 21

ballplaying and ballcourts 12,
  66, 79, 133
bark-paper books 11, 13–14
Berlin, Heinrich 68
black (*ik'*) glyphs 125
Bonampak', Stela I *142*
breath (*ik'*) glyphs 127
brush pen, use of 13, 94–95,
  154
buildings and structures
  132–33

calendar 37–58, 167;
  calendrical signs 26, 27, *140*;
  formulae and tables 167
Calendar Round 40–44,
  47–48, 51, 59, 93, 170, *141*,
  145, *148*
calligraphy, carved and
  incised 14
"captives" title glyph 77
"capture" glyph 89, 90–91,
  170
Caracol, tutelary deities 109
carvers 13, 95–96
Catherwood, Frederick 7
cave drawings, Naj Tunich
  150
censers 134
ceramics: artists' signatures 95;
  depictions of gods 12–13;

painted animals 129;
painted vase (Nak'be style)
  151; "Resurrection Plate"
  153; texts 14, 98–107, *see
  also* pottery
ceremonies *see* rituals
Chaak (rain and lightning
  god) 12, 60, 108–109,
  110–11, 123
Chak Chel 117
Chiapas language 15
Chich'en Itza 11, 134;
  Lintel 4 (Las Monjas) *146*
Ch'olan language 15, 16, 77
Ch'olti' language 15, 129
Ch'orti' language 15, 62
"Classic Mayan" 15–16, 47,
  62; grammar 26–36
Classic Period 11–13, 14, 15
cloud (*muyal*) glyph 127
codices: calendrical glyphs 56;
  picture and text linkages
  14; survival of 11, *see also*
  Dresden; Madrid
Collier, Mark 7
color-directions 123
colors 125–26
compound glyphs 17–18
conflation 26
consonants 9
consonant-vowel-consonant
  (CVC) 20
Copan 13, 15, 36, 46, 47, 62;
  Altar Q 57; calendrical
  inscriptions 169, *140*;
  censers 134; Stela I 46, 47
costume and adornment,
  glyphs for 135–36

Date Indicators 32–33, 37, 93
dates: Distance Numbers
  and 37, 40, 53–55, 59, 169;
  eclipse calculation 53;
  royal births 59–61;
  Supplementary Series
  glyphs 49–53, 170
day-signs 40, 41–42
death and burial, of rulers 62
death gods 119–20
directions 123–25
disharmony, rule of 21–22

Distance Numbers 37, 40,
  53-5, 59, 169
Dos Pilas 63; Stela 15 63–64
Dresden Codex 38, 87; deity
  glyphs 111, 114, 115, 117,
  119–20; numerals 40;
  omen texts *154*

earth (*chab/kab*) glyphs 127
East, direction glyphs 124
El Perú 96; Stela 34 95–96
Emblem Glyphs 68–71, 74,
  78, 110, 121, 171
engraved bones, Burial 196
  Tik'al *149*
ergativity 16, 29

family relationships 86–88
Fox, James 16

gender: agentive nouns
  28–29, 128; lack of 15,
  26–27
glottal stops 9, 21, 155
gods 109–120, *153*, *154*
green (*yax*) glyphs 126
grid system 17–18
Grube, Nikolai 74, 79, 97

Haab (365-day "year") 40,
  42–44
Hero Twins 12, 13, 75, 116,
  140, *153*
Houston, Stephen 15, 22, 68,
  71, 132
humans, glyphs for 128
Hunahpu 12, 75, 116
Hun Ajaw 12, 116
Hun Hunahpu 116

inflection 26–27
Initial Series 37, 38, 44,
  48–50, 51, 170, *143*
Initial Signs 99, 171, *151*
inscriptions: carved and
  incised 11, 14; cave
  drawings *150*; ease of
  reading 14; language
  of 15–16
Introductory glyphs 48, 54,
  169

Itzamnaaj 12, 109, 113–14

Janaab Pakal, King 62

Kalak'mul 11, 12
K'awiil 12, 63–64, 109, 112
K'inich Ajaw 112–13
Knorosov, Yuri V. 20, 32, 89,
    156, *154*

Landa, Diego de 20, 26, 35,
    43, 78, 94, 109, 112, 156
Lexicon 161–66
life-cycle events 59–62
lintels 14, 64, 77, 134;
    Chich'en Itza *146*;
    Tik'al *147*; Yaxchilan 46,
    47, 92, 170, *138*, *139*
locative prepositions 35–36
logograms 18–20, 161–66;
    with phonetic
    complements 24–25;
    polyvalence and 25–26
Long Count 11, 40, 44, 45–52,
    55–56, 59, 63, 93, 167, 170
Lords of the Night series 65,
    167, 168, 170
Lounsbury, Floyd 87
Lunar Series 37, 50, 51–53

Madrid Codex 111
Maize God 12, 116, *153*
Manley, Bill 7
Martin, Simon 74, 79
Maya civilization 11–13
Maya languages 15–16;
    grammar 26–36; lexicon
    161–66; polysynthetic
    nature of 16; syntax 16, 27
Maya glyphs: comparison with
    Egyptian 8; conflation 26;
    reading order 17–18;
    transcription conventions
    19, *see also* Syllabary
Maya script 17–36; principles
    of 17–20
Maya texts, decipherment 7,
    8, 9, 14
Monkey-men twins 13
month signs 43–44
morphosyllabic signs 22–24,
    156, 161
mountain/hill (*wits*) glyphs
    127
murals, painted 14

Naj Tunich Cave, drawing 52
    150
names, of rulers 74–85, 170
name-tagging 103, 132, *149*
Naranjo 60
nicknames, of rulers 74, 79
North, direction glyphs 124
nouns 27–28; agentive 28–29
number system 38–40

"The Paddlers" 118
Paired Gods 118
Palenque 15, 72, 132; Palace
    Tablet 46, 47; sarcophagus
    62; Tablet of the 96
    Hieroglyphs *144*; Temple
    XIX *145*, *148*; Temple of
    Inscriptions 136; Triads
    109, 111, 118–19, *145*
parentage glyphs 86–87
"Pawahtuun" 13, 99–100, 109,
    115, 123, 171
Period Ending 56; rituals
    63–64, 170, *141*
Peten region (Guatemala) 11,
    63
phonetic complements 18
physical world, Maya view of
    123–27
Piedras Negras 49, 58, 59, 61;
    Altar 2 93; Stela 3 49;
    Stela 10 58; stelae 49, 58,
    61
place-names 36, 68, 71–73
polyvalence 25–26
pool (*nab*) glyphs 127
Popol Nah facade 36
Popol Vuh 12, 13
positionals 16, 34, 42
Post-Classic period 11,
    13–14, 15
pottery vessels 135, *see also*
    ceramics
prefixes 161; Set A pronouns
    34
prepositions, locatives 35–36
Primary Standard Sequence
    (PSS) 95, 99–107, 135, *151*,
    152, *153*
Primary texts 98
pronouns 15–16, 29–31;
    possessives 16; Set A
    29–30, 32, 34; Set B 30–31,
    32, 34
pronunciation 8–9

Proskouriakoff, Tatiana 59,
    61
pyramids 12, 62, 133

Quiriguá: Stela D *140*;
    stelae 38

rain (*ha'*) glyph 127
red (*chak*) glyphs 126
relationships *see* family
    relationships
religion 12–13
"Resurrection Plate" *153*
rituals 12, 63–67; astronomy
    and 37; bloodletting
    64–65, *138–39*; calendrical
    13; conjuring 170; god
    impersonation 65; Period
    Ending 63–64, 170, *141*;
    royal dance 12, 65–66
Robertson, John 15, 22
royal lives 59–62
rulers: accession of 61, 169,
    171, *145*; death and burial
    62; divine origin of 12;
    list of 79–84; names 74–85,
    170

sacrifices 12
Schele, Linda 65, 167
Schellhas, Paul 108, 110, 112,
    115, 116
screenfolds 13
scribes and artists 13–14, 18,
    72, 94–97
Secondary texts 98
Seibal *141*; Stela 10 *141*
siblings, glyphs for 88
signatures: ceramic painter's
    95; sculptor's *138*, *142*
sky (*kan*) glyphs 126
society, structures of 12
software programs 8, 37, 168
solstice points 123–24
South, direction glyphs 124
spouse (*y-atan*) glyph 87
stelae 14, 37, 133–34; Arroyo
    de Piedra *143*; Bonampak'
    142; Copan 46, 47; Dos
    Pilas 63–64; El Perú
    95–96; Piedras Negras 49,
    58, 61; Quiriguá 38, *140*;
    Seibal *141*; Tik'al 170;
    Yaxchilan 40, *see also* stone
    monuments

Stephens, John Lloyd 7
stone monuments 11, 133–34, *see also* stelae
Stuart, David 15, 22, 28, 61, 64, 68, 71, 97
stucco glyphs, Palenque *148*
suffixes 161; morphosyllabic 22–24, 25, 27–28; plurals 28; Set B pronouns 30–31, 34
Sun God 12
supernatural world 108–22
Supplementary Series, date glyphs 49–53, 170
Syllabary 155–60, *see also* Maya glyphs
syllabic grid *see* Syllabary
syllabograms 18, 20–22, 25, 32, 161, *146*
Synharmony, Rule of 20–21, 31

temples 12; Palenque 132, 136, *145*, *148*; Tik'al *147*
Teotihuacan 76
Thompson, Sir Eric 7, 15
Tik'al 11, 12, 14; engraved bones *149*; Stela 16 170; tutelary deities 109; wooden lintel, Temple I *147*
time, and the calendar 37–58, 123
titles 74–79, 170; of scribes and painters 94–97

tombs 13, 14, 62, 133
"Toothache Glyph" 61
"toponyms" 36, 68, 71–73
translations 19
transliteration 19
Triads (deities) 109, 111, 118–19
"tzolk'in" 41
260-day Count 40, 41–42

Usumacinta drainage sites 94

"Vague Year" 42
Van Stone, Mark 8
vases: Altar de Sacrificios Vase 122, *152*; Nak'be style painted vase *151*
verbs 31–36; aspect 16; and calendrical signs 27; Date Indicators 32–33; intransitive 15–16, 27, 29, 31–32, 32–34; passive forms 32, 59; positionals 16, 34, 42; tense 16; transitive 15–16, 27, 29, 31, 32, 34–35
voiceless aspirates 9, 21
vowels 9; syllabograms 20–21

warfare 89–93, 170–71
war leaders (*Sajal*) 77
"Water Group" glyph 109–10
way spirit companions 12–13, 121–22, 129, 133, *152*
West, direction glyphs 124

white (*sak*) glyphs 125
wind (*ik*) glyphs 127
"Wing-Quincunx" sign 99
women: deities 117–18; (*ixik*) glyphs for 128, 171; spouse (*y-atan*) glyph 87; titles 75, 77, 79
world trees 123
writing materials 13–14

Xibalba (Maya Underworld) 62, 119

Yaxchilan 60, 64, 134; Lintel 8 92; Lintel 14 *139*; Lintel 24 *138*; Lintel 29 170; Lintel 48 46, 47; Stela 12 40
Yaxha 72
Yax K'uk' Mo' 13
yellow (*k'an*) glyphs 125
Yukatan 11, 123
Yukatek language 15, 16, 129; Long Count names 46–47; month signs 43–44; Motul Dictionary 29; orthography 8–9

Zauzich, Karl-Theodor 7